BOOK in
a MONTH

BOOK in a MONTH

the foolproof system for writing a novel in 30 days

Victoria Lynn Schmidt, Ph.D.

WRITER'S DIGEST BOOKS
Cincinnati, Ohio
www.writersdigest.com

For more fine books from F+W Publications, visit www.fwpublications.com.

12 11 10 09   5 4 3

Distributed in Canada by Fraser Direct, 100 Armstrong Avenue, Georgetown, ON, Canada L7G 5S4, Tel: (905) 877-4411. Distributed in the U.K. and Europe by David & Charles, Brunel House, Newton Abbot, Devon, TQ12 4PU, England, Tel: (+44) 1626 323200, Fax: (+44) 1626 323319, E-mail: postmaster@davidandcharles.co.uk. Distributed in Australia by Capricorn Link, P.O. Box 704, Windsor, NSW 2756 Australia, Tel: (02) 4577-3555.

Visit our Web site at www.writersdigest.com for information on more resources for writers. To receive a free weekly e-mail newsletter delivering tips and updates about writing and about Writer's Digest products, register directly at our Web site at http://newsletters.fwpublications.com.

Library of Congress Cataloging-in-Publication Data

Schmidt, Victoria Lynn
  Book in a month : the fool-proof system for writing a novel in 30 days / Victoria Lynn Schmidt.
      p. cm.
  Includes bibliographical references.
  ISBN-13 978-1-58297-486-6 (hardcover : alk. paper)
  1. Fiction--Authorship. I. Title.
  PN3365.S36 2008   2007037998
  808.3--dc22

Edited by Kelly Nickell
Designed by Grace Ring
Production coordinated by Mark Griffin

fw
F+W PUBLICATIONS, INC.

DEDICATION

To Dixie, Dusty, Oliver—

And the four-legged angels I have yet to meet.

ACKNOWLEDGMENTS

Thank you Jack Heffron for taking a chance on a new writer all those years ago, and to all my editors at Writer's Digest: Kelly Nickell (*Book in a Month*, 2008), Michelle Ehrhard (*Story Structure Architect*, 2005), and Meg Leder (*45 Master Characters*, 2001). Thank you for your help and guidance.

And, as always, thank you to my family.

ABOUT THE AUTHOR

Victoria Lynn Schmidt (www.charactersjourney.com) is the author of *Story Structure Architect* and *45 Master Characters*. She graduated from the prestigious film program at UCLA, holds a master's degree in writing from Loyola Marymount University, and holds a doctorate in psychology. She also attended film school at NYU and studied independent filmmaking with some of the top artists in the field. When her writing schedule allows it, she teaches English and screenwriting at several universities around the country.

TABLE OF CONTENTS

INTRODUCTION

It's always too early to quit.

—Norman Vincent Peale

In *The Book of Secrets*, Osho, the great teacher/philosopher, said something regarding creativity and spirituality that I have always felt could help writers, if I could just find the right forum to make it accessible. Though the exact quotation is about meditation, I have paraphrased the wisdom to make it applicable to writers. You see, we have this view in life that everything can be learned, that everything is about finding knowledge and then we will be happy. While this may be true for some things such as science and medicine, it is not true for art and creativity. These things you must experience for yourself. You must have a direct connection to the development of a thing, the creation of it. You cannot sit at the feet of Shakespeare or Maya Angelou and walk away an author.

Likewise, you cannot read a book on writing and then—"poof!"—become an author (though books *are* great guides). No. You must experience the act of writing to be an author. You must experience things for yourself. The only way you can do this is to write, from beginning to end, a story. And then do it again and again and again. Then you will have the experience; *then* you will be an author.

This BIAM 30-day system is designed to help give you that experience. It will show you how to face your blocks, develop a worthy goal, and stick to it with checklists to keep you on track. But you have to be willing to participate in the experience. You have to understand that, above all else, you are giving yourself an experience here: the experience of what it is like to write, to create.

HOW TO USE THIS BOOK

This book is set up to be the one and only resource you will ever need to write (and then rewrite) your manuscript. Everything about this particular story and characters will be contained within these pages.

You will probably use a fresh copy of this book for each project you work on, because the book is meant not only to be helpful, easy to use, and motivational, but also to be a constant companion along the way. Pick up a new blank copy of this book, fill out the worksheets, place the name of your project on the spine (via the enclosed stickers), and you have your "mobile writing office" with you wherever you go. No more lost ideas or disorganized notes. Finally! Writer's Digest worked very hard to design the book this way, so thank them for it!

You will also want to re-read the introductory chapters before beginning this and all subsequent BIAMs ... after all, studies have shown that it sometimes takes seeing something three or four times before it sinks in!

If you absolutely must set your project aside for a few weeks, this book is set up so that you will be able to come back to it without wasting time figuring out what you were doing, what your new ideas for the story were, or where all of those important notes and reminders are—*What was that character's nickname?*

I can't tell you enough how valuable this aspect of this book has been for me. Try as I might, I could not find a good system for organizing my fiction projects in any store. (Of course, I've had to put my fictional work on hold from time to time to write these creative writing books, but I have truly created the very books I'd needed and looked for, books that will assist and further my—and now *your*—career as a writer.)

A quick and easy reference guide with checklists, worksheets, and a free companion e-group are all part of the program. You can use this program to:

- write a manuscript in 30 days;
- write a detailed outline in 30 days;
- rewrite a manuscript in 30 days;
- work on all the blocks and issues that come up as you attempt to reach your goal (more on this shortly).

Since I have received numerous letters from readers asking how they can merge the techniques from all my creative writing books, I will occasionally refer to my previous books, *45 Master Characters* and *Story Structure Architect*. These two books work very well with *Book in a Month*, but you do not need them to use this one. As a writer, I wrote the books I wish I'd had as references on my private writing bookshelf. For example, the female hero's journey and new male hero's journey in *45 Master Characters* and the different story structures in *Story Structure Architect* can be easily used with this book. Acts I through III of the traditional structure are outlined at the start of each week, as it is in those books, so you only have to correlate each act between books.

GOALS AND TIME MANAGEMENT: SUPPORTING YOUR MOTIVATION

We all have issues to deal with that keep us from fulfilling our goals. Any big undertaking will bring those issues to the surface in the form of resistance. Resistance is the way your subconscious tries to protect you from taking risks. Ever get really tired the second you tried to change a habit? Sudden fatigue is a great indicator that resistance is at play. (Later, you'll see eight tips for effective time management; after that, I'll give ten steps to overcome resistance in your own work.)

There's also a chapter on goals—and the importance of selecting the right project that aligns with those goals—because so many otherwise-productive writers end up wasting time on projects that just don't fit them or their interests at all.

How can you stay motivated to finish a project if you subconsciously hate it (or feel lackluster about it) from day one? Trying to write for the market is a no-no! Don't do it. Even if you finish your manuscript *today*, it still won't be on store shelves for another one to three years at the earliest. The markets will most likely change by then.

Now let's take the first step and answer some of the questions that may be floating through your head just from reading the title (that nasty little inner critic scares easily):

- **Has anyone written a book in 30 days?** Yes! I know a group of genre authors who do just that—ever hear of Nora Roberts (a.k.a. J.D. Robb)? Or how about Dame Barbara Cartland? She wrote a book a week, becoming one of the most prolific writers in history.

- **Yeah, but how good were those books?** That's a judgment question (and we'll take a closer look at the role our inner critic plays in the writing process later in this introduction). We don't have time to judge the work of others because that only leads us down the path to judging our own work. Drop "judging" from your vocabulary! There have been great and horrible books in every genre, whether they took 30 years to write or 30 days. Nora Roberts is constantly on the *New York Times* best-seller list! Besides, it's unlikely that your 30-day manuscript will emerge fully formed, ready for the printing presses as is. That comes with skill, practice, and a lot of polishing ... but you can't start down that path to the rewrite unless you have a complete manuscript ready to work with.

- **If I can't find the time to write now, how will I find the time to write a whole book this quickly?** Short deadlines can actually be invigorating. What I mean by this is, if you tell yourself that you have to set aside six months to get a draft down, it will seem like a huge task (will you really ask your family to make a sacrifice for six months?). But what if you only have to ask your family to pitch in for one month? Do you see where I'm going here? If 30 days does not seem like much to write a book then, hey, 30 days is not a big sacrifice. Give it a shot. The kids, family, and friends can pitch in for that amount of time without too much strain. More importantly, you'll have given yourself a very narrow, and hopefully focused, time frame in which to work.

- **What happens if I start to feel isolated and alone?** Don't worry; this book comes with a free companion e-group list, which we'll discuss shortly. Sign up, report your progress, and talk over problems with others who are doing the same thing.

- **Can this book help me rewrite my manuscript if I've got a finished one that I really want to try to salvage?** Yes. As you read the book, you will see tips and weekly wrap-ups specifically for those who are rewriting an earlier draft instead of starting a new one.

- **I understand what you are saying, but what if I am just blocked?** This book covers writer's block and demystifies it. You are the source of your own blocks, which means you have the power to eliminate them. Stop resisting and go for it. Numerous working moms and overextended college students have done it!

- **So how can I do this?** I will discuss the five most important keys to getting a book done in 30 days. The worksheets keep you on track and help you make sure you are moving forward in the best way possible. The information you need is within these pages. Just follow along.

FIGHTING OFF YOUR INNER CRITIC

I won't kid you: The biggest obstacle to accomplishing this goal is your own inner critic and personal psychology (more on this later). I will do my absolute best to help you be a successful writer, giving you all the information and techniques I can, but you have to put your butt in the chair and start typing. I can't do that for you. We are all different, and our needs change as we grow and develop as writers, so use what works for you. But be open to new solutions, techniques, and exercises. I have included many of them to choose from throughout the book.

Besides, in the end it really doesn't matter how "good" or "bad" your manuscript turns out to be … first drafts are first drafts, no matter *who* writes them! Instead, it is all about the journey. You're reaching for a lofty goal, and as you meet and face down your blocks and your resistance, many of you will find that what you've learned along the way has helped you to grow in more ways than just as a writer.

BIAM ONLINE SUPPORT

It is my job to gently guide you, the writer, into the fascinating new world of writing a book in a month. If you need a little extra support, you're always welcome to join the free companion e-group at http://groups.yahoo.com/group/VBIAMClub to become part of a vibrant discussion community. There, we'll keep each other positive and motivated. You can even share your weekly successes by posting your answers to the tasks given each day or week, but that's entirely up to you. Daily prompts telling you what to work on each day are also posted there, assuming you start on day one of the month.

"Lurking" on the VBIAMClub discussion community is okay but not encouraged. The more you participate, the more you will get out of it. The more you are involved, the higher your commitment is. The more people you announce your goal to, the more you will feel the need to write. You can post your weekly totals there and stay accountable!

You will find your fellow writers in the group are very helpful and friendly. If you are worried about copyright issues, then don't post anything too specific, but get those goals and word counts posted. Announce to the world what you will do so you feel compelled to write. The whole point of the group is *motivation*! Come help others get through their 30 days; they'll do the same for you.

Check in with my Web site at www.CharactersJourney.com to see new offerings and resources, or just sign up for our announcements newsletter to receive an e-mail (usually one or two per quarter) when new things are happening.

Never underestimate the power of the group mind. I encourage you to sign up for this book's free companion e-group, VBIAMClub, and to communicate with your peers. You are all facing the same challenge, and the collective energy of a group can help you break past innumerable blocks.

Other Online Groups

A while ago, I heard about the National Novel Writing Month, or Nanowrimo (www.nanowrimo.org), and an assortment of other online Book in a Week (BIAW) groups. These groups, in different ways, gather together writers who all have the common goal of finishing a word count or book in a certain number of days. The idea is that, by stating your goal, having others hold you accountable, and creating a deadline, you will get that book written.

These groups are wonderful, and they help a lot of writers write more than they ever have before. The problem is that many writers come to these groups with their bad habits, blocks, and inner critics in tow, so many writers don't meet the intended goal of the group. I wanted to create a program to help the majority of writers out there reach this goal. There's nothing wrong with needing a little help. I ran my own group online and participated in some of these groups myself. Yes—I personally wrote novels in 30 days, and it was exhilarating each time!

NO MORE STALLING!

This is a fast-paced, intense world, but when you have a guide, such as this book is meant to be, you will find fun instead of stress. After all, you've set out to do something few ever risk doing—accomplish your dream. You will finish that novel and give life to your characters, and you will do it in 30 days' time. It may not be a perfect manuscript, ready for publication, but it will be a completed manuscript.

Just imagine for a moment that your manuscript is finally written. Go ahead—visualize your completed manuscript right now. Doesn't that feel great? Many writers have written a book in 30 days; some have done it in one week. So commit to your project, and to yourself, and let's get started!

THE FIVE SECRETS OF BIAM

Our deeds determine us, as much as we determine our deeds.

—George Eliot

Is it really feasible to write a book in 30 days? In a word: yes. But there are five secrets you need to know beforehand in order to be successful. Few books or courses that profess to teach the art of "quick drafting" actually teach these five secrets, which makes it very difficult for the writer to actually produce his or her draft. In truth, these five secrets might seem, at first, very simple, but once you begin to apply them, you will see why these are necessary not just to keep your book moving, but to keep it moving *forward*.

The first three deal with techniques, tools, and tricks you can use to maintain forward momentum and focus. The last two deal with the writer him- or herself; there is a bit of *psychology* here.

The five secrets to successfully writing a book in a month are:

1. work "as if"
2. leave out subplots
3. be realistic
4. examine your self-esteem
5. trust yourself

SECRET #1: WORK "AS IF"

Working "as if" means that you keep writing—that you keep moving forward with your story—without stopping to rewrite every time you change your mind about a character, plot, or setting detail. Instead, you take notes on your Story Tracker worksheet to stay on task while still remembering changes you'll need to make later. You see, as new ideas or new directions come to mind, you jot them down—in an organized ways of course—and keep writing *as if* you've made those changes already. There is an excellent reason for doing this, one that every 30-day writer should keep in mind:

> **You cannot write and rewrite at the same time if you want to finish a book in 30 days.**

Now, all of the changes you come up with while in the process of writing are no longer taking up valuable space in your brain, and you are free to keep moving forward, free to generate more ideas, free to keep getting those pages done. Your new ideas and revision notes can be stored safely on the Story Tracker worksheets until you have finished your first draft without interruption. To keep things organized, it is best to break your notes down by *act*—a traditional three-act structure consisting of beginning, middle, and end (or setup, development, and climax/resolution)—and then supply specific details under the following categories: character, plot, subplot, and setting. Let's take a closer look at what such notes might consist of.

Character

Let's say for some reason you want—or, more likely, *need*—to change the name of your character from Anne to Barbara, and you want her to be a pianist instead of a waitress. Instead of going back and changing every page that contains a reference to Anne or her occupation, instead you jot down on the Story Tracker sheets:

Change Anne to Barbara and make sure she's a pianist in all of her scenes, check pages 3–42.

Then you do the obvious: You use the name Barbara from this point forward and write as if she is a pianist.

Likewise, you can keep similar notes for changes to a character's background. If you need, for example, to change the childhood issues for one character so you can make her "gritty and jaded" when she goes home for Christmas, make the appropriate "marker" on your Story Tracker sheet and write her as if she were "gritty and jaded" from this point on. This type of change may—and probably will—affect other characters, like her parents, so make sure to note any implications the change might have in terms of relationships between characters, motivations, histories, and so on ... all concerns for you to address *later*, in revision.

If this seems at first to be too-obvious advice—perhaps a bit too easy or too hard, depending on your temperament—consider the reason for addressing character changes in this way: You've reached a problematic point in your story, a point where the story has dictated a change must be made, and you've *made* it. Now, rather than retreating to your previous pages to make meticulous corrections—essentially "bookkeeping"—you are free to explore the possibilities presented to you by your story ... the very possibilities that necessitated the change in the first place.

You are free, in other words, to write.

Plot

You are absorbed in your writing, and all of a sudden you realize you should have included a fight scene between Chris and Mike two chapters ago. It is the only way this current scene you are writing will make sense. No problem. Jot down on your Story Tracker:

Fight scene between Chris and Mike in chapter 2. The outcome is X because Y. The point is Z. See page 132.

You can also get out your red pen and write on the page you wish to include this scene:

Insert fight scene here—see Story Tracker notes.

Whew! This is such a quick way to get that idea down and keep moving forward. Think about it: If you stopped right now to write out that whole fight scene, how much time would it take you? Are you the type of writer who might get sidetracked by it? Sometimes we go back to change one thing and then find our minds wandering toward new ideas on top of new ideas. This is classic writing self-sabotage! Don't let that happen; just keep your notes, keep them clear, and keep moving forward.

Subplot/Situation

You suddenly get an idea for a great subplot. Or you know you desperately need a subplot to keep the story moving forward while you convey information, but you don't want to write it in just yet. (In the next secret, you will see that writing your whole subplot out in this stage is not ideal, anyway.) Use the Story Tracker either to jot down this fantastic subplot idea or to note that you'll need to find a fantastic subplot for this scene later on:

Add subplot: Cherry (the heroine's sister) betrays Kevin, once again leaving the heroine to break the news to Kevin and deal with the fallout.

Or jot down that you need to create a subplot here and why you feel you need one:

This scene is very slow, yet I need to convey this information to the readers. A subplot could spice it up a bit. I could use that quirky waitress from the bar in Act I to cause a lot of trouble for the heroine.

Either way, jot it down on your Story Tracker so you can go back later—in revision—and add any preliminary pieces needed to set up the subplot in the previous chapters. Subplots usually don't affect the plot in a big way, but if your subplot does, then you need to put that information on the worksheet as well. Be careful that it doesn't become part of the main plot; you don't want two stories going at once:

Perhaps the heroine gets into more trouble in the main plot because she talked to Kevin in the subplot? Maybe we don't know who Kevin really is?

But again, even if you have a dynamite idea for a subplot that would fit perfectly, at this point in your writing, you simply want to turn to your Story Tracker sheet and record it, not begin writing it. Why? Because you're writing a book in a month—remember?—and, in order to do this, you'll need to follow the advice in Secret #2.

STORY TRACKER

ACT I				
Character	Plot	Subplot	Setting	Other

ACT II				
Character	Plot	Subplot	Setting	Other

ACT III				
Character	Plot	Subplot	Setting	Other

SECRET #2: LEAVE OUT SUBPLOTS

Many writers churn out a quick version of their stories with subplots to be added later. This really depends on your writing style and level of mastery. Most of us do better if we can just focus on the main characters and plotline, and race through to the end. There is nothing wrong with that. So feel free to leave out the subplots for now.

As you write, you can keep track of what subplots you might return to in revision:

Add subplot: Cari meets with hero to plan the surprise party Alex doesn't know about.

And then continue on with the main plot. This way, you know where you want the subplots to fit in and how they will progress, but you don't waste a lot of time and brainpower working on them just yet. Why not go ahead and write them? *Because subplots are always the first to go, or change, during a rewrite.*

Once you get to the end, you will be able to see:

- where the story is a little slow;
- where things don't make sense;
- what new information needs to be added; and
- how many characters need to be changed or dropped.

Can you see that working too much on subplot can be a waste of time? Even if you keep all the basic subplots you create during these 30 days, they will still change; the main plot will *require* them to change because it will change and grow as you write—new settings, new characters, new information, new transitions, new purpose, new goals, new subtext. The subplots will have to reflect these changes. Don't waste your time, unless it is absolutely necessary. You're in charge here, so do what you think is best. Just know that it is okay to forego the subplots when writing a draft in 30 days.

SECRET #3: BE REALISTIC

Most of all, you need to be realistic—if you work two jobs, have kids to care for, and have health issues, don't push yourself to finish a book in 30 days. Instead, resolve to complete a story synopsis. A synopsis is an unstructured outline. You work out the beginning, middle, and end and develop characters and their goals. You also work a lot on your opening lines and hooking readers.

You can write anything within this 30-day time period. Be gentle on yourself and your creativity will continue to flow.

> **Set a goal too high and the creative blocks will be more difficult than ever!**

Be careful about getting too upset about setbacks and delays. Remember, one bad day can become three, and three can become ... well, you get the idea. Then you might find yourself dreading the process and finally giving up. Don't let yourself have a bad day. Try to find the bright spot. Stay positive.

Recognize Your Obligations and Distractions

It's important to go into this 30-day process with a clear understanding of what you can and can't give to it. It's also important to recognize the difference between balancing your obligations and using life's little distractions as an excuse. Take a look at the questions below. Are you:

- in the middle of a major move?

- in the middle of a break-up, having relationship problems, or getting married soon?

- recovering from an illness or addiction?

- possibly losing a job (or did you lose one recently)?

- starting something new, like a job or career?

- about to have a baby?

- overextended with family commitments?

- unsure where your next meal is coming from?

- about to go on a major vacation?

- facing the death of a family member or beloved pet?

- already committed to the PTA and the Scouts and the car pool and ... and ... and ...?

Answering "yes" to one or more of these questions doesn't mean you should put off writing. It just means that you should cut yourself a little slack—you're going through a lot. Set your goals accordingly, and be realistic about your goals during the 30 days. Follow along and resolve to write a detailed outline. This way, you are working on the acts and getting to the end, just like everyone else is, but you are working on a short—meaning a manageable—outline.

> ## For the rest of you ... FIND THE TIME AND JUST DO IT!

SECRET #4: EXAMINE YOUR SELF-ESTEEM

Never guilt or shame yourself into writing, or put yourself down too harshly for not writing. Guilt and shame never helped anyone's self-esteem, and self-esteem is what you need to complete a book in a month.

Self-esteem allows you to commit to your goals, and it allows you to make time for what is important to you. Self-esteem means you can say to yourself, "I matter, and so do my goals." If you are having a very hard time with this, there are a number of books out there on enhancing your self-esteem. You may want to take a look at some of them and see if they help. It's okay to be dedicated to others in your life, but you still have to take care of your needs. Sometimes setting a good example is the greatest thing you can do for your loved ones.

Many kids would prefer to have a happy, fulfilled mother to a fancy home-cooked meal.

If you agree with *more than two* of the following statements, your writing self-esteem could use a boost.

- I blame someone or something for not being able to write.

- I constantly blame myself for not writing enough, even if it's not my fault.

- Instead of finding time to write, I do what others want even when I don't want to.

- I don't express myself enough in my writing to avoid upsetting, hurting, angering, or offending someone. ("What would my family say if they read this?")

- I allow people to critique my work before it is ready to be critiqued.

- When someone criticizes my work, I feel like they're criticizing me.

- I am jealous of successful writers, or I'm easily angered by their success.

- I secretly want my writing peers to fail so I won't be left behind.

- I'm reluctant to set and announce my writing goals for fear that I won't attain them or that I will be ridiculed.

- When I tell people I'm a writer, I feel special.

- I use this "writer" identity to feel better about myself, so my self-worth relies on me maintaining it. I can't fail in any way as a writer.

- I'm filled with big writing dreams and goals, but I just can't get started or follow through.

- I give up at the first hint of rejection.

- I make excuses for my work before I show it or read it out loud. ("This is just a draft; I'm not finished with this scene yet.")

- I'm embarrassed to send my work out or to have others read it.

- I don't really know what I want from my writing career. ("Why bother?")

- I hear myself saying "yes, but" when talking to other writers about opportunities.

- I feel like I have no control over my time and how I spend it; writing is always pushed to the wayside.

- I really don't see that I have many choices in life to do what I want to do.

Boost your self-esteem by focusing on your strengths. Don't criticize your work or allow others to do so. This is why many writing teachers tell you to stay away from negative people when writing and keep your work to yourself in the beginning. Listen to them! Once you have finished your manuscript and are happy with it, you can then sort through criticism from others. Until then, keep your work to yourself. Or tell the person looking at your work you only want positive feedback for now.

You need to feel entitled to your special 30 days of writing. Yes, this is special! You need to feel as if it is your right to have these 30 days. You need to stand up for yourself. Writing down your feelings can help you to crystallize what really matters to you. Give it a try, and answer the following questions now:

How will you feel if you are on your deathbed and never even gave writing a real shot? Will you feel as if you got all from life that you wanted to get? Will you feel like you missed out on something meaningful?

What events in your life do you remember fondly? (Being in the school play? Helping a classmate? Getting good grades? Being selected for an honor? Making people feel better? Going to college? Raising great kids? Rescuing an animal? Getting in to some program or course?) Why do you think these events stand out in your memory? Recalling areas of success in your life and focusing on them can keep you moving forward now.

What goals have you already achieved in life? List everything—even if the accomplishments aren't writing-related. We're boosting your self-esteem here, so everything counts. After all, there's just no time for doubts during this 30-day time period. If you were successful before, you can be successful again.

SECRET #5: TRUST YOURSELF

Here's the big question: *Do you trust yourself?* Sometimes we don't achieve our goals because we devalue our capacity to deal with whatever may arise when reaching for them. Trusting yourself may be the greatest gift you can give and receive. When you stop the worry by saying, "I trust myself to deal with whatever comes up," the anxiety lifts away. Here are some remedies to ward off the most common writing worries:

- **What if this manuscript isn't any good?** Even if that were the case, you have the ability to rewrite it. Trust that you did your best. If you honestly do your best, there should be no room for regret.

- **What if I get rejected?** Don't see your manuscript as an extension of yourself; instead, trust that you will be able to deal with rejection if it happens. Trust yourself to honestly recognize when rejection is constructive and when it is hurtful. Learn from constructive criticism and do better next time.

- **What if I can't reach the goal?** Sometimes, it's easier—and more comfortable—to sabotage yourself and blame others. When you actively prevent yourself from succeeding, it's easier to accept failure. Instead of working against yourself, if you don't reach your goal, then trust that you will take an honest look at the reasons why this happened and adjust your goals for next time. Don't simply beat yourself up over it.

- **What if I feel really anxious about this 30-day task?** Trust yourself to deal with whatever may come up these 30 days, and then just go for it. Really now, what is the worst that can happen? You won't finish a manuscript. We're not talking life and death here!

Most of our writing blocks come from lack of self-trust, pure and simple. We wouldn't get upset, worried, angry, accusatory, or anxious if we trusted ourselves to deal with whatever might come up, in any situation. So, visualize yourself dealing well with your biggest writing fear (perhaps rejection) right now. Imagine how you will handle it and overcome it.

> **Every day is a new day, a new chance to begin again.**

If you need to repeat one of the 30 days, then that's what you need to do. Give yourself permission to mess up one day, and make it a good one! Does that take some of the pressure off?

We all have lives to lead; we all have reasons for not writing. The next 30 days are going to test your dedication to becoming an author, so if you can't articulate why you're writing, then you just might run in to trouble. To prepare you for this, let's pause here to explore your motivation and commitment to writing:

Why do you *want* to write?

_____

Why do you *have* to write?

_____

How will your life be different after you finish this manuscript? What will change?

_____

How will your life be different after you finish three manuscripts? (Will you feel like a "real" writer?)

_____

How will you feel about yourself after you finish this manuscript? (Will you have more confidence?)

_____

How will this feeling help you accomplish other things in life?

_____

TIME MANAGEMENT

Guard well your spare moments. They are like uncut diamonds.
Discard them and their value will never be known. Improve them
and they will become the brightest gems in a useful life.

—Ralph Waldo Emerson

This brings us to time management. If you have trouble with it, then
tough. That's right, I said it—tough! Too many writers use lack of time
as an excuse not to write. When you say you don't have the time, what
you are really saying is, "Something else is more important right now
than writing."

Is that really true for you? Are all these other tasks you're completing truly more important to you than writing? If so, then stop
beating yourself up about not writing and put this book down. Writing has to be a priority for you, at least for the next 30 days. I know
you're probably thinking, "I have to feed my kids and take care of my
family! How could she say this?" To this, I would respond: You absolutely cannot say you don't have the time. All authors have to learn to
balance their time.

Remember in the last chapter where I discussed how you might
have some new, extenuating circumstance holding you back right now?
That is not what we are talking about here. We are talking about the
regular routine—your daily, weekly, monthly, and even yearly priorities.

We are talking about why you may have been stuck working on one manuscript for several years, never getting to the end—or, even worse, why you've been stuck writing the beginnings of several stories but never finding the time to finish one of them.

Many parents with a thousand things on their to-do list find time to write; writing is just number one thousand and one. Seriously. Nora Roberts had a lot on her plate when she started writing—still does—and yet she's found the time to pen more than a hundred and fifty novels. How does she, or how does any author, take on the daily duties of life and of writing at the same time?

Successful authors manage their time, pure and simple.

Get a small notebook and take it everywhere you go. Write down *everything* you do. This will help you see where your few precious moments of free time are and allow you to schedule your writing time. With this helpful exercise, you'll be able to find—or make—time to write.

There are also many great books and Web sites out there on time management, so start studying how to better manage your time. Get yourself a weekly or monthly calendar and plot out how to make the BIAM process work for you. Use the eight time management tips included in this chapter, as well as the worksheets in this book, to help keep you focused and on target as you continue on this 30-day journey and beyond.

TIP #1: MAKE WRITING THE FIRST THING

The easiest way to create a new habit is to make it one of the first things you do each day. As each new day progresses, you can be pulled in a number of different directions. There are simply too many distractions that come on once the day is set in motion, not to mention the fatigue that can overcome you after lunch.

What you *resolve* to do first thing—or at least early in the morning—you *will* do. It is so much easier to sit down and write a page or two and *then* conduct your daily business than it is to check e-mail, pay bills, return phone calls, wash your hair, wash your dog, and get pulled into half a dozen different tasks before trying to write a page or two. This is why many people exercise first thing in the morning. For the next 30 days, your exercise is writing.

TIP #2: ADHERE TO THE PARETO PRINCIPLE

Have you heard of the Pareto principle, or the 80-20 rule? It is the principle that 20 percent of your time and effort generates 80 percent of the results, or that 80 percent of what you accomplish is caused by 20 percent of your effort. Most things in life were found to be distributed this way, like the distribution of wealth: 80 percent of all the money goes to 20 percent of the people. Another example is the number of writers to the percentage of total books sold: 80 percent of books are sold by 20 percent of the authors.

So, if 20 percent of your effort causes 80 of your accomplishments, wouldn't it be great if you focused on that 20 percent of result-getting effort 100 percent of the time? Of course it would! Think of all the free time you would have if you only had to do a fraction, the most effective part, of the daily, too-often-unproductive grind. We all waste time and effort every single day. We do things that will get us nowhere, and that won't yield any value in our lives. This stuff takes up 80 percent of our effort if we let it. This means that as you embark on your BIAM, you must:

- drop all that busywork that gets you nowhere;

- drop all the clients who don't add to your business and do eat into your writing time;

- drop all the negative friends who drag you down;

- drop the agent who is holding you back;

- drop all the manuscripts you don't really love, or those that you started just because you thought they were marketable;

- drop all your high expectations (you don't have to have the cleanest house on the block—one writer was spending six hours every Saturday cleaning her house, and she had no kids or pets!); and

- drop whatever you find is within that 80 percent of wasted effort—focus on that result-getting 20 percent of effort.

When you focus on things that don't truly matter to you, you are working within the 80 percent of effort that won't get you the 20-percent results you want. How could it?

We have so much more time available to us now than at any other time in history; it's just that our thinking is flawed. There was a time when women spent ten hours doing the laundry by hand; now, we just pop it into a machine. Where did those ten hours go?

Studies show we actually have too much time available to us, and we squander it.

We fill our days with meaningless tasks. Read *Living the 80/20 Way* by Richard Koch (www.the8020principle.com), and your eyes will be opened:

> We have never been so free, yet failed to realize the extent of our freedom. We have never had so much time, yet felt we had so little. Modern life bullies us to speed up our lives ... but going faster only makes us feel like we're always behind.

Simplify your life and start focusing on the 20 percent of your activity and effort that gives you the 80 percent of your happiness and results, at least for 30 days.

Don't get confused here—this principle is not about being fast, but about slowing down and focusing on what is important to you. If you want to go to the country (your goal), you can go via the quick, less scenic route or the longer, more picturesque one. Both routes fit in with the 80-20 principle—if you like to drive fast, then take a fast route; if you like to enjoy the scenery, then take the scenic route. You create your goal and then get there in the way that uses your skills and interests … your 20 percent.

If you force yourself to go via the scenic route when you really love speed, you will be unhappy because you won't get there fast enough; thus, the scenic route becomes part of your 80 percent of wasted effort. The trick, then, is to know both your "to-do" and "not to-do" list, to know your wants as well as your don't-wants.

You want to write a book (it's your goal—or you wouldn't be reading this book, right?), and doing it in 30 days is the route you want to take. Focus on this every day for the next month and you will be happy! How wonderful will you feel when you hold that manuscript in your hands? Eliminate your 80 percent of wasted effort. You do have the time … at least for one month.

TIP #3: KEEP TRACK OF YOUR WRITING TIME

Keep track of your writing time every day using the following Writing Time Tracker. Make it a habit to write in the number of hours you spend on each area for one project over 30 days. You can also plug in word or page counts in "Totals."

When you sit down to write, note the time; when you are done, jot down how long you worked in each category. The "Miscellaneous" category is for research, reading, writing exercises, buying materials, and other writing-related tasks. Use the "Distractions" category for all the non-writing distractions that come up during your set writing time.

WRITING TIME TRACKER
Time Spent Writing Per Day

Project Name:

WEEK 1	1	2	3	4	5	6	7	Totals
Miscellaneous								
Outline								
Act I								
Rewrite								
Word Count								
Distractions								

WEEK 2	8	9	10	11	12	13	14	Totals
Miscellaneous								
Outline								
Act II								
Rewrite								
Word Count								
Distractions								

WEEK 3	15	16	17	18	19	20	21	Totals
Miscellaneous								
Outline								
Act II								
Rewrite								
Word Count								
Distractions								

WEEK 4	22	23	24	25	26	27	28	Totals
Miscellaneous								
Outline								
Act III								
Rewrite								
Word Count								
Distractions								

TIP #4: DON'T ASK FOR TIME

Don't ask for time for yourself. If you ask, people can say no. If you just do it, then you've done it and you've got it. Your being happy is the only change they'll notice.

—Dr. Mira Kirshenbaum

Just find the time any way you can and take it. Of course, I don't condone lying or cheating to get the time you need, though some writers have stretched the truth a bit. The point Dr. Kirshenbaum is making in the above quote is that, while writing may be important to you, few people in your life will see it as important. Many will just see it as an unnecessary indulgence. Asking them to help you find time for writing just won't work. If you had a major circumstance or emergency, these same people would give you all the time you needed, so the time is there. They just might not see writing as worthy of it.

You have to decide writing is worthy of that time, and then just take it.

One writer had more than three months of sick and personal leave saved up at his day job. His boss wanted him to use some of it before he lost it. He was afraid to take off, but he did, and now he has a small but steady writing career in the works.

TIP #5: MAKE APPOINTMENTS WITH YOURSELF

Henry Kissinger once said: "There cannot be a crisis next week. My schedule is already full." For many of us, things that aren't scheduled just don't get done. We sometimes live from appointment to appointment, trying to squeeze little tasks in between. In fact, without an appointment, some of us just don't know what to do and often fall victim to another person's request. So, make an appointment with yourself so you can fill that free time with writing.

When you have concrete plans with yourself it is much easier to say *no* to others. You don't have to make up excuses. "I have a 1 P.M. appointment" is fine to say to someone without any explanation needed. Only you need to know what, when, and where you are going. There is no room for negotiation here. The impulse to give up your writing time is not as strong when you have it written down in your calendar as an appointment. Just hoping time will magically materialize out of thin air is not an effective strategy.

Appointments tell your creative brain that writing is important. They also tell your muse to get ready: Work time is coming.

TIP #6: BUY YOUR TIME (LITERALLY OR FIGURATIVELY)

Check out this pearl of wisdom from Dr. Mira Kirshenbaum's *The Gift of a Year: How to Achieve the Most Meaningful, Satisfying, and Pleasurable Year of Your Life*: "Use money to buy time by using money to get people to do things for you that will save you time … . Whatever it costs you, spread out over a lifetime it isn't that much." Okay, maybe you don't have tons of money to get babysitters, eat out, and hire maids, but could you barter for some of these things? Ask for favors? Agree to babysit next month for another mother if she babysits this month for you? Could you afford to eat take-out three times this week? What about frozen dinners? Can you whittle your cleaning routine down to a bare minimum, once-a-week chore?

Just think about this for a minute. How much money is spent on hobbies, goals, and entertainment in this country? Billions of dollars! Yet when it comes to finding the time to write, we are reluctant to spend any money at all to do it. Why is this? Most hobbies, desires, and activities cost something to partake in it. And these things usually are not part of our lifelong dreams and goals. They most certainly don't have much of a chance of giving us a return on our investment as writing may do for us. So what's the problem here?

One writer I know spends eighty dollars a month on a haircut, yet he can't imagine splurging on a new notebook to jot down his ideas. Something is off here. For thirty dollars a month, he could have a new laptop computer to write when he has to travel for work, but there is no way he will ever buy it. It's all about choices.

Remember the financial gurus out there talking about foregoing a latte every day to put that money in the bank? If you stopped treating yourself to that daily latte, you would have more than one hundred dollars extra cash every month. Imagine if you factored in the price of a daily muffin. That would be more than *two* hundred every month. What is your "latte" expense? Make it your writing expense now.

It's not how much money you make, but how well you manage it that makes a difference. We have all heard about the secretary making $30,000 a year retiring a millionaire, while the executive who spent his whole $250,000 yearly salary couldn't retire if he wanted to. Just look at a compounded interest chart and you will be mad at your parents for not socking away a thousand dollars a year in your name as a kid! You would have retired a millionaire from a total of $10,000 invested.

And if you don't have the extra money to literally buy your time, then get creative with it. For example, one writer I know saw that she spent two hours a day preparing, cooking, serving, and cleaning up from family dinners. She decided to spend the Saturday before her BIAM cooking chicken cutlets and lasagna and freezing them for the family to thaw out during her 30 days. Low and behold—she found herself two hours a day. Her husband even agreed to pick up dinner on his way home from work twice a week to help her out. What a great guy!

TIP #7: GET OUT THE AX

Every time someone or something comes into your life, hold it up to your list of priorities and see if you still want to talk to that person or do that activity. Talking to your angry, gossiping neighbor for an hour can't hold any allure when you realize it takes away from your family and your writing goals. Learn to prioritize—that will help tell you where you should be focusing your efforts. What is important to you? Do you spend enough time on it? Why?

I know a writer who realized she spent four hours a day watching TV. She never saw it before, but logging her time made it clear. Were watching soaps and talk shows worth not finishing her manuscript? "No way!" she said. "They weren't even that interesting." (She's now happily published and occasionally records her favorite shows to watch at night.)

Write down a list of your main priorities so you will know where to draw the line when requests are made for your time:

Now that you know your priorities in life, write down a list of things that take up your time and are not on your priority list:

Can you get rid of the things that aren't priorities? If not, can you make small appointments to do these things so they don't take up too much of your time? Can you delegate them to others?

TIP #8: JUST SAY NO

Why do so many of us have trouble just saying no? Because most of us have been programmed to say yes, to be a people pleaser. Usually the problem is that we are afraid of conflict. We think, "What will this person do or say if I don't help out?"

Well, if you can't stand conflict in life, then you sure won't be able to write conflict on the page. Conflict is what stories are made of, so get used to it. Enjoy it. When writers can't stand to do bad things to their characters, they usually are terrified of conflict. These writers rarely have successful careers. Be assertive!

This tip is also all about sticking to your guns, because once you say no to someone, you have to stand firm. If you backpedal at all, you will lose all momentum for saying no again in the future. Be true to your word and to yourself. If you say no, it means no.

Also be careful of maybes. Sometimes we feel guilty for saying no, so we instead decide to say maybe to get out of an uncomfortable situation. Don't do it. Maybes only lead other people on. It leaves them thinking there is hope and that they can wear you down. It also shows them that you devalue your other commitments and aren't sure of yourself. Always say no firmly and directly. If you really feel bad, say, "No, not until next month when I am finished with a current commitment. Please feel free to check in with me next month."

RESISTANCE

What you have to do and the way you have to do it are incredibly simple. Whether you are willing to do it is another matter.

—PETER F. DRUCKER

If you are a productive writer and you're reading this book for a little boost, then you won't need to read this chapter ... but the information is still great to know.

Every time you commit to a goal, there will always be a part of you that resists obtaining that goal (and attempting to write a book in a month is a pretty hefty goal, at that). This part of you wants to protect you from taking risks, from changing things, and from moving too far out of your comfort zone.

Perhaps as a child you were led to believe that if you excelled at something, people would be jealous and not like you anymore. Or perhaps you're afraid to succeed at something because you will over-shadow your parents and excel where they failed. And maybe an even more common fear is that of the "sophomore slump," or having a great success and never being able to achieve that level again. There are numerous reasons someone would subconsciously resist reaching a goal.

If you think resistance is holding you back from making a commitment to writing and the BIAM program, and you are not sure why you are manifesting it, it doesn't matter. What matters is that you recognize that what you are feeling is not about thinking that you might be working on the wrong project, or that maybe you really aren't a writer, or that you are a procrastinator by nature, or any of the other excuses you might be clinging to. Know that you are instead simply resisting your goal and that you need to allow yourself to feel uncomfortable for a while. Think of it as growing pains. But still keep on working. Work through those feelings. Ignore them as best you can and keep going. They will go away.

Here are some common signs you are in writer's resistance:

- You're always too busy to write.

- You have a history of procrastinating on every story you attempt to write.

- You want others to tell you what to write next.

- You feel as if you can't write without a partner.

- You lose interest in your current story and keep finding new ideas to pursue.

- You're completely disorganized when it comes to outlining your story or cleaning up your workspace.

- You fog up or space out after writing the first act.

- You feel paralyzed when you sit down at the computer.

- You're impatient ("Why do I have to read this book? I just want to write already!"), and you beat yourself up for not finishing enough work.

- You keep running into negative people who deter you from writing.

- You tell people all about your ideas before you've given yourself a chance to develop them.

- You often feel irritable when you think about writing or feel like you're losing control—over your story, your writing time, etc.

The fact of the matter is that most of these excuses are self-afflicted. You feel like you are surrounded by negative people because you are—you attract them! You tell people your ideas, telling yourself it'll clear things up in your own head, when really, the more you talk, the less you work, and the less excited you get. Abandoning these defensive measures can feel like taking a huge risk.

Taking a risk implies loss of control; otherwise there would be nothing at risk. When you start this 30-day system, you are taking a risk, the biggest risk being: *What if I fail? Will that mean, once and for all, that I will have to give up my dream of being a writer?*

We know consciously this is not true, but that subconscious alarm is very, very protective. Perhaps you can quickly outline a second or third story and tell your subconscious this current manuscript is just for practice!

If you are experiencing persistent resistance, you need to ask yourself the following questions:

Why don't I want to finish this manuscript?
_____

What will happen to me if I finish it?
_____

Why should I let myself write this manuscript?

_____

If you're having trouble coming up with answers, force yourself to dig a little deeper (you've got to get a handle on your resistance now so that it doesn't become an obstacle during your BIAM). Try completing the following sentences:

I'd love to start this 30-day plan, but ...

_____

If I became a great author ...

_____

I can't finish an entire manuscript in 30 days because ...

_____

I _can_ finish an entire manuscript in 30 days because ...

_____

If I did finish this manuscript, I would feel ...

_____

It's all about finding the core of your resistance, which is really a fear, and re-framing it. Do some journal writing if necessary. Take some time to explore this issue.

There is also the possibility that you may be "demand-resistant." This is when you resist doing anything that feels like you are "being told what to do," even if you are the one giving the orders. The subconscious is a tricky thing. Ask your subconscious this question: *Is it in my best interest to avoid writing?* Of course not.

"Having no time" is not a valid excuse. It isn't. You have to be willing to face the discomfort of making a change in your life. Even if you have published a book before, you can still meet resistance. Resistance can ruin a career before it ever gets started.

Even if you believe you've worked through all of your resistance before, and even if this is your third time completing this book, you should still check for and guard against resistance using the questions on the previous pages. New things come up for us all the time.

10 STEPS TO OVERCOME RESISTANCE

Once you've identified the roots of your resistance to writing, you can overcome it. Here are 10 sure-fire steps to help you break on through. (And guess what? This book's built around these very steps, so I *know* you can follow them.)

1. **Create an outline.** Working within a structure helps you stay focused. BIAM provides the outline for you. Use the fold-out sheets to chart your progress.

2. **Break the writing down into small, doable tasks.** BIAM breaks down all of these tasks and provides advice and exercises to support the process.

3. **Know the next step.** This will keep you from feeling so over-whelmed and confused.

4. **Hold yourself accountable.** The VBIAM online group will help you with this one. Tell your peers on the Web list your goal and they will do the same. You can then support each other and hold each other accountable. There are also numerous goal-setting Web sites where people state their goals for all to see.

5. **Gather support.** Look into joining a writing group (the VBIAM online group can also help here). Or start your BIAM program at the same time as a fellow writer and then cheer each other on. Or you may be lucky enough to have your family and friends to cheer you on. Remember, you, your fellow writers, and your supporters are all in this together.

6. **Be specific.** Articulate your goals (and remember to be realistic). BIAM forces you to state the goal as "to finish a draft in 30 days" instead of "to write a book someday." Being specific about your goals is the only way to know how to go about achieving them and the extent to which they've been met.

7. **Visualize the entire goal from start to finish.** This is no time to try to wing it. You've got to stay focused, and planning out exactly how you're going to achieve your goal is essential to your writing success. BIAM has handy charts to help you do this. Keep them visible.

8. **Create a deadline.** This is an easy one—30 days is your deadline. (Some people say the *only thing* you need to write a book is a deadline.)

9. **Celebrate your successes.** Staying motivated is crucial here. Even the smallest achievement is worthy of acknowledgment.

BIAM has a task section on Day 9 for creating a reward for yourself to help you through the final push.

10. **Make it a habit.** They say it takes 30 days to break old habits and instill new ones. Write every day for 30 days, and *writing* will be a new habit. When your BIAM project is over, you will have the success of 30 days of writing under your belt. It will be that much easier for you to start and complete your next project.

If you still find yourself struggling, try using the delay technique. This involves waiting ten minutes to one hour before giving up. If you sit down to write but want to walk away and give up, say to yourself: *I will give up in ten minutes, but for now, I will sit here.*

You will be amazed. Either you will start writing or you will have demonstrated, at the least, your commitment. Even if you give up, you will still *feel* like a success because you took some sort of action to help yourself. You did *something* different this time. You took a step toward breaking a bad habit.

REAPING THE REWARDS OF SUCCESS

Let's list some of the benefits of reaching your goal to write a draft in 30 days: Will you feel like a real writer? Will you be able to pursue an agent with an air of confidence? Feel more capable in general? Identifying the benefits of completing your BIAM project will be one more motivator you can rely on over the course of the next 30 days.

When I finish this manuscript in 30 days ...

WHAT'S YOUR SIGN?

Select benchmarks that will show you, your subconscious, and your friends and family that you have made great progress, and write them down. Perhaps making it to page 150 would make you feel like you are really on your way. Or making it to day ten would make you feel like a success, and the rest of the month would just flow after that. Whatever it is, give yourself concrete signs that things are progressing well. Perhaps resistance will leave you after a few of these signs have come to pass.

My writing benchmarks are ...

Decide how you will face your resistance battles. How much do you really want to finish this manuscript? Do you want it bad enough? If not, are you sure you're telling the story you really want to tell?

The next chapter will help you answer these questions and define your goals.

SETTING AND KEEPING GOALS

Great minds have purposes; little minds have wishes.

—Washington Irving

It is extremely important for any self-employed person to set concrete goals. This is especially true for creative professionals. Make no mistake about it: As a writer, you are a self-employed creative professional. You create a product (a manuscript) and try to sell it. That is a *business*, and all businesses need a plan. Writing down your goals is the first (and most important) step to formulating one.

As writers, we always seem to have ideas bouncing around in our heads. If we chased after every one of those ideas, we would never get anything accomplished. Just think for a moment about how long it takes to get a book out there—to get an idea, write, rewrite, rewrite, get an agent, get a publisher, rewrite, find a press, and make that triumphant visit to the bookstore. Exhausting, isn't it?

Do you really want to spend that much time working on something that does not fit in with your goals? Do you want to waste your precious 30-day BIAM on a project you don't deeply care about? Where will you be when you have completed such a book? Not much closer to your goals, that's for sure, and probably not that successful, either. Unless, of course, you just want to publish for the sake of publishing. This is fine, but usually it is not a very rewarding route to take. Will you really "sell" and promote such a book if it isn't in line with your goals or where you want to go as a writer? Not really; you will just find yourself battling resistance yet again.

If you don't have real goals written down, how will you get anywhere in your career? You know the old saying: Fail to plan, and you plan to fail.

It really is true; ask any successful person, and she will tell you that once she wrote down her goals, things really started to happen. Somehow putting things down on paper makes them real. The subconscious mind is really impressed by it and will usually fall in line and help out. Writing down your goals also makes you think deeply about them. Self-improvement guru Gene Donohue puts it another way: "The difference between a goal and a dream is the written word."

KNOWING YOUR PASSION

The first step in choosing the right project is to figure out who you are as a writer and what kind of project you want to work on. This means figuring out what you're most passionate about and working that passion into your story, whether you choose to write a bone-chilling mystery, a steamy romance, or something more literary. It is important to do this *before* developing your story idea because your passion will—or should—have a direct influence on the idea. Why? Just think about it for a minute. There really are no shortages of ideas. It does not take much to come up with one. You cannot copyright an idea because it is not, by itself, uniquely yours. No, it is the *execution* of that idea that makes all the difference, and that is where goals come into play. Your goals should be detailed enough to ensure that the type of project you pursue reflects who you are and what you want your story to encompass.

I always ask my students to write down their goals, and, in most cases, the first attempt is a little too general. For instance, on her first try, one student wrote:

I will write three books this year.

This is way too broad. It doesn't reflect what this writer cares about at all, and that's very important information to simply leave out. On her next try, she wrote:

I will write three mysteries that inspire readers to speak their minds and take charge of their lives.

This is specific, but not too confining. Speaking her mind is important to this writer. At the same time, she understands what her core idea/theme will need to be. No matter what type of story she writes (horror, comedy, romance), she will need to have an inspirational element that inspires readers to speak their minds and take charge of their lives. Once she works that in, the story will be uniquely hers. She will feel passionate about it, even if it is a horror story and she hates writing horror stories (like when her agent hired her to write one). She will have no problem doing book signings and giving interviews because she loves the book. She will even have something passionate to say about it: "It's a horror story, but more than that, it teaches the reader to speak her mind and take charge of her life."

Take a few minutes to think about the things—the values, the characteristics, the beliefs—that matter most to you:

What are you passionate about?

Book in a Month

What gives you energy and motivates you?

What keeps showing up again and again in your stories or the stories you love to read?

If you don't have a firm understanding of what you're passionate about, developing your writing goals can be very hard to do. You've got to tackle the big questions: *Who am I? What genre should I specialize in? How do I want to be remembered?* Many writers have never even considered these questions. The answers to these and other questions help you find your own unique way to execute story ideas. If you want to stand out in the slush pile, this chapter is extremely important, so pay attention. Let's take the answers to questions you just completed and go a little further:

What is important to you creatively? Do you want to educate? Entertain? Scare?

Do you have a personal cause or agenda that defines you? (Feminism? Animal rescue? Global warming?)

What types of books do you enjoy? Movies? Music?

What types of stories did you like as a child?

Once you've identified your passions, it's time to start figuring out how to express them in your story. Remember, if you have an emotional connection to the material you're writing, it will be that much easier for you to stay invested over the long haul and reach your goals. Beth Mende Conny, a wonderful writing coach and founder of WriteDirections.com, came up with the following exercise that I have found to be very helpful in capturing the essence of a story idea:

THE ROCKING CHAIR RULE

Imagine yourself older, not just by a few years, but by decades. You're on a porch in a rocking chair, rocking slowly but enjoyably. It's a lovely day—bright, warm sun, knock-your-socks-off blue sky; the kind of day that makes you want to sit and rock forever.

Lazily, your eyes sweep the horizon, the vast expanse of grass that gentle flows into a distant range of soft, welcoming mountains. You're feeling peaceful, reflective as you think back on this gloriously crazy but interesting thing called life.

You remember all you've done, from first steps to first kisses to the first time you realized you were a grown-up. You draw to you the faces of those who touched your life, softened its rough edges, those you loved with an aching heart.

You think of favorite places and things: your room as a child, a piece of jewelry still tucked away in a bedroom drawer. Your mind sifts through these memories as if through a box of photographs, each a vivid reminder of where you've been, what you've done, and who you've become. You understand that you won't be in this rocker or on this porch forever. Life passes quickly ... too quickly.

But with this bit of knowledge comes another—you know now, in a way you've never grasped before, the importance of leaving some part of yourself to the world. You know that you were put on this earth for a reason, and while you may not know the answer in full yet, you know that in part, your purpose was in some way fulfilled by the writing of your book. You remember it with pride—how writing it demanded your best, making you draw on strengths you never knew you had.

You remember, too, that while your book may not have changed the world, it touched lives. Certainly, it touched yours. It was, as you now know, your way of leaving your mark on the world, your way of saying, "I was here. I mattered."

The title of that book was: _____,

And it was about:_____

_____.

This is a beautiful exercise, and by writing the title and what your book was about, you now have some idea of who you are as a writer. You don't necessarily have to write this book now. In fact, you may never write this manuscript. This exercise is about getting in touch with the elements of who you are as a writer. Within your answer you will see certain topics, genres, ideas, and directions that best suit you.

DEVELOPING YOUR STORY IDEA

> If your success is not on your own terms, if it looks good to the world but does not feel good in your heart, it is not success at all.
>
> —ANNA QUINDLEN

As your passion and story idea merge, be careful you don't limit yourself. Let's say you want to write a book that's about "a strong heroine who overcomes obstacles and learns to love herself." This doesn't mean you have to write chick-lit; it just means that maybe your stories, even if your genre (or editor) calls for a male action hero, should have strong heroines in them, as well as women who overcome obstacles. Can you write a fantasy with this? Yes. Can you write a horror novel with this? Yes.

The answer you provided in the Rocking Chair Exercise, which may evolve over time as *you* evolve, is the core idea and theme of your work. It is what really interests you enough—and therefore motivates you—to put your butt in the chair and write.

Now that you have some insight into who you are as a writer, answer the following questions to see if your current project represents a blend of your passions:

If you had to describe your work as a whole in a single line, what would that line be? (Heartfelt stories that make you cry? Smart, steamy romances? Hardcore heroes who risk everything?)

How would you like your work to be remembered?

Which genre is best for your writing style and interests?

Does your current project meet most of your answers to the above questions? Is this project in line with who you are as a writer? If you like romance and adventure but are trying to write a sad drama, I have to ask, *Why?* You can do this if you want to, of course, but you should know that you may have some trouble getting it finished. Agents, publicists, and publishers also want to know this about you. They want to know what makes you different from all the other writers out there. They also want to know how to market your work. They want something they can sink their teeth into: "This writer is known for creating stories that educate as well as entertain her young readers."

WRITING THE BOOK YOU WERE MEANT TO WRITE

If you are aware ahead of time that you may be working on a story that is not in line with who you are as a writer—say, if you've been contracted to write in a genre you're unfamiliar with—then you can compensate for it not only by giving yourself more time to complete the story, but also by recognizing blocks and resistance as they come up. That way, you will understand why you feel blocked, and you can then either write the story anyway or give yourself permission to shape your storyline so it fits better with who you are as a writer. It's called *slanting your project*, tweaking it a bit to get more of "you" into it. Many writers who work for hire do this. They will take any writing job they are offered, but they immediately pick through the idea and inject their own ideas and themes into it. This is what makes us unique, what adds style to our work. Knowing what projects *not* to become involved in, as well as what projects to pursue, is the biggest key to a fabulous writing career.

Do you think Nora Roberts and Barbara Cartland would have been so prolific if they wrote in a vastly different genre and topic area? Most likely, they would have slanted any book they wrote into the mold of who they were as writers. This is why you can take any story idea, give it to ten different writers, and get back ten different versions of it! Who you are as a writer will always come through your work. Accept and embrace that.

Now that you know who you are as a writer and what is important to you, take that information and turn it into an overall career goal in first or third person. For example:

- I want to write X stories with Y and Z. (*I want write sensual stories with suspense and intrigue.*)

- X and Y are what writer Z is all about. (*Spunky heroines and slapstick comedy are what writer Jack Doe is all about.*)

Does any of this sound familiar? It should! You have all been told that you need to boil your ideas down into a one-sentence pitch. Well, this is the one-sentence pitch of yourself. It is just as important to pitch yourself as it is to pitch your story. You don't want to be a one-hit wonder. Pitching yourself tells people about your career; pitching your book just tells them about that one book. Now you try it:

One-Sentence Pitch
_____

If Jack Doe is hired to write a horror novel, he can create a spunky heroine with one or two slapstick moments and make the story his own.

He won't struggle as much in the beginning to write this horror book because he knows what he likes to write about. He knows what will make this an enjoyable experience for him. Can you imagine how he might struggle if he couldn't put his finger on what he didn't like about this horror project? Instead, he can jump right in with suggestions and ideas for the publisher. (Remember, this statement about who you are as a writer may change over time. That's okay.)

BUILDING YOUR BIAM GOALS

Now that you've taken the time to identify your passions and expand your story idea, you should have a project you're excited about and personally invested in. This project should allow you to construct and achieve goals that you know you'll keep as write your way through the next 30 days. Before we get too far, though, here are a few crucial tips on goal setting:

- Make sure your writing goal is something you personally want for yourself. Make sure it is your goal and not something you think you have to do to become successful, like write for the current market trends, or write something because your mom always wanted you to write it. (Uncle Joe's life may be funny, but is it three-hundred-pages funny? Do you care?)

- Make sure your writing goals don't work against each other. You can't write epic novels *and* expect to write five novels a year.

- Make sure your writing goals don't work against your life in general. You can't write twenty romance novels this year if your other goal is to travel the world by boat with five friends.

- Always create positive writing goals. Write what you *will* do, not what you won't.

- Keep your writing goals specific, but leave some wiggle room for creativity.

- Actually *write down* your writing goals!

- Revise your writing goals as you grow and develop as a writer. Every six to twelve months is good, though you will do it more often in the beginning.)

As you establish your BIAM goals, start small so you don't get overwhelmed. Just write down your core writing goal for the next 30 days. Make it simple and easy to accomplish. Then if you reach your goal, or even surpass it, you will have given yourself a nice confidence boost.

The way you go about reaching this core BIAM goal is to break it down into weekly increments—it will seem much more manageable this way. Then, break it down into daily goals and see that there really may not be as much to do per day as you thought there was.

Want to write one hundred pages in a month? That seems like a lot ... but it's really twenty-five pages a week, or, better yet, about three or four pages a day.

SAMPLE GOAL TRACKER

Goal	Course of Action
80,000 words in 30 days	20,000 words a week (3,000 a day)
100 pages in 30 days	25 pages a week (4 pages a day)

This doesn't seem like too much, and if you happen to miss a day, well, you've only fallen behind by three pages. Surely there's no reason to beat yourself up over that!

In this 30-day system, you should aim to accomplish 25 percent of your goal each week. At the end of the month, see how you have done. If you easily made your 300-page count, then next time shoot for three hundred fifty. If you had a tough time with it and only wrote fifty pages, then you just set your goal a bit too high and need to either change something in your life to make more time for writing or accept that you can only get about fifty pages done in a month and embrace that as your writing goal. (Though you might also consider if you're either in resistance, and should thus re-read that chapter.)

Regardless of what you are writing or rewriting, it's important for you to determine how many pages you realistically want to have completed by the end of the month. How many pages is that per week? (While page counts and three acts are what the 30 days are all about, you can articulate your goal in the form of a word count if you want to.)

Let's face it, we can all get to "The End" if we only write a five-page story. (I know that trick!) So having page or word counts as part of your goals helps a lot. When things get tough and you feel like giving up, you can tell yourself that you only have to write four pages today. Write them as quickly (and as horribly) as you need to, but write them. If your goal breaks down to two pages a day ... well, you really can't argue much with that. You could write those during commercials. No excuses.

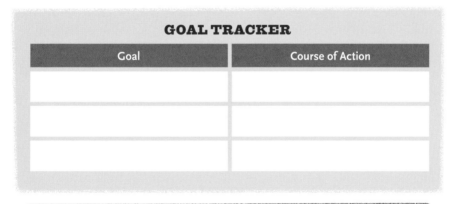

GOAL TRACKER

Goal	Course of Action

Make a Collage

If you are a visual person and would like some more inspiration, then make a collage showing images of successful writers and other things that represent success to you. Use colored paper or plain computer paper—do whatever you want, just don't put the 30 days on hold to find the perfect items for this collage. Do this as quickly as possible.

You might decide to post pictures of your favorite *successful* author (whether famous or not, this author wrote and published). Go to your favorite author's Web site and print out pictures from there. Have a favorite book that inspires you? Set it out, or print out a copy of the cover and hang it up. You can even find some images of yourself, paste them on top of these pictures, and write headlines for them about how successful you are. Put some of these images in places where you will see them often, like your bathroom mirror or near your computer screen.

SHARING YOUR 30-DAY GOAL

Make sure you only reveal your 30-day goal to those who will encourage you. Some friends and family members will always see you as you used to be—the "non-writer." It is very common for a family unit to discourage change among its members, even if it is for a member's benefit. When one member changes, it can stir up too many things for the others. They may be forced to look at areas of their lives that they have yet to change for themselves. Many people will fight this sort of self-exploration. Be sure to surround yourself with supportive allies as you embark on your BIAM project. You can always post to the VBIAM e-group list or look for writing groups online or in your area. Of course, not all writing groups are positive. You have the right, and the responsibility to yourself, to walk away from any group that is not supportive.

I will share my 30-day goal with:	I will not share my 30-day goal with:

Please know that regardless of anything else, it is wonderful to share your goals and dreams with others after you have established some strong roots and have a sense of who you are as a writer. There will be other people who will want to help you keep moving forward. One goal always leads to another one, and you never know who may help you take your career to the next level. But in the beginning, you are very vulnerable, so be careful.

As the saying goes: A little child can knock down a sapling oak tree before it has grown strong roots, but once the oak has grown tall enough, almost nothing can knock it down. Establish your roots first, then go out there to network and let others share in your dreams. Be decisive and assertive. What worked one day may not work the next, and some people who have been allies may all of a sudden become less so. Just thank them and move on without judgment. You don't have the time to hold grudges or get upset.

SIGNING YOUR BOOK CONTRACT

This next exercise is probably one of the most important exercises in this book. It is a contract between you and your muse, between you and your book, between you and your future readers. It is a binding contract.

Tear out this contract, read it out loud, sign it, and hang up where you will see it every day.

BOOK IN A MONTH CONTRACT
Book Title: _____

I, _____ , agree to follow the steps of the 30-day Book in a Month system.

I will make the necessary changes in my life to accommodate this goal, and I will ask family, friends, and my fellow writers for help when I need it. I will organize my time well so I can do this, and I will set aside all non-essential tasks so I have time to achieve my goal.

I will work on my book _____ days a week (if I miss a day, I'll just keep going). I will complete _____ words/pages and get to the end. No matter what happens during these 30 days, I will just keep writing.

"I don't have the time" is not a good enough excuse for the next 30 days.

I promise myself that I will celebrate when the 30 days are up, even if I only met 75 percent of this goal. I will tell my family and friends to get ready for this celebration in Week 3, to further motivate myself.

This book is important to me. My future readers are waiting to read it and I owe it to them to finish it. What I have to say is important.

Signature: _____

Date: _____

THE BOOK IN A MONTH SYSTEM

The person who makes a success of living is the one who sees his goal steadily and aims for it unswervingly. That is dedication.
—CECIL B. DEMILLE

Now that you have gone over the preliminary notes and advice, it is time to jump in and start your Book in a Month. Make sure to complete the previous chapter on goals. It is extremely important, so do not skip it.

In the following sections, you will find a separate chapter for each of the four weeks of the BIAM system. Just follow along, fill out the worksheets, and keep writing, no matter what happens in life, even if it is only a few paragraphs a day. Focus on *one* story—the one you selected in the earlier chapter on goals—and remember: One copy of this book equals one story.

As you will see, there are a few extra days depending on the length of the month you choose to use for your BIAM, so you have one or two extra "emergency" days at the end if needed; missing one day during a week won't ruin everything because you've got one or two extra days built in to catch up. Just don't rely too heavily on catching up. Let those be for emergencies only. Save them.

These four weeks are set up to complete story acts:

• Week 1: Act I = 25% of goal

- Week 2: Act II, Part 1 = 25% of goal
- Week 3: Act II, Part 2 = 25% of goal
- Week 4: Act III = 25% of goal

With this system, you'll be sure to keep structure in mind and plan accordingly. There is nothing more frustrating than reaching 60 percent of your goal only to realize you are still setting up the story in Act II. Using the acts in this way helps you avoid that. Publishers, especially genre publishers, have page count requirements. You can't just decide to write a 600-page manuscript. Plan ahead and watch your act breaks.

Many times, a writer is great at writing Act I and will go on and on, setting everything up, while another writer loves to get to the end and will breeze through Act I in a race to get to the good stuff. Segmenting your writing time over these 30 days into acts helps you avoid these mistakes. It also helps those of you who don't want to outline. These writers can just jump in without an outline, knowing where they should be by a certain word or page count. If they are writing a 200-page story, they know they should be done setting up the story by page fifty, at the latest. This way, even without an outline, they won't go off on tangents and mess up the flow of the story or miss their page count. Again, we are using the acts as guideposts.

One note: There is a small contingency out there telling new writers not use the three-act structure. Of course, this kind of statement gets a lot of attention. Usually they are defining the three-act structure in a very different way from "beginning, middle, and end," as we do here. Anything can happen within these acts, so don't get sidetracked debating semantics; you have too much writing to do. Just get a draft on paper.

Remember, actually finishing the story is most important. If your goal is to write 80,000 words, that is wonderful. But you could easily write 80,000 words without ever getting anywhere near the ending, so the acts help you stay on task. For instance, 80,000 words could mean:

- Week 1: Act I = 20,000 words
- Weeks 2 and 3: Act II = 40,000 words
- Week 4: Act III = 20,000 words

How you break it down is up to you and might also depend on the genre you are writing for, but guidelines are always helpful. You don't want to find yourself at 35,000 words and still setting up the story. The acts are guideposts to manage your word and page counts.

WEEK 1: ACT I

During Week 1, you will fill out nine worksheets and complete Act I, focusing on story, your goals, building the conflict, and Act I's turning point.

WEEKS 2 AND 3: ACT II

During Weeks 2 and 3, you will fill out eighteen worksheets and complete Act II, focusing on checking the plot, developing some subplots, motivating your protagonist, watching for genre elements, and crafting the Act II turning point.

WEEK 4: ACT III

During Week 4, you will fill out seven worksheets and complete Act III, focusing on checking the story for holes, developing final obstacles, setting up character arcs, and constructing the climax of the story.

Let's get started!

Take a deep breath …

Smile …

And visualize a completed manuscript.

BIAM 30-DAY CALENDAR

1	2	3	4
Welcome to Week 1: Act I • Write a one-sentence story summary. • Map out your central story idea.	• Summarize your ten essential scenes.	• Start your At-A-Glance outline. • Begin to take notice of what you'll need to research.	• Learn more about your characters using the Character Story Sketch, Character Snapshot, and Character-Revealing Scenes worksheets.

5	6	7	8
• Identify and develop your Act I turning point.	• Explore each character's backstory and decide what to include in your story.	• Take a look back and identify any weaknesses in your story. • Finish Act I. **25% Completed!**	**Welcome to Week 2: Act II, Part 1** • Stay solution-oriented as you head into Week 2. Don't get distracted or bogged down!

9	10	11	12
• Plan your post-BIAM celebration—this is an excellent way to stay motivated! • Speaking of ... make sure your characters are properly motivated.	• Check the stability of your plot with a quick snapshot. • Maintain your story's tension by adding in solid cliffhangers whenever possible.	• Brainstorm new twists for your plot, characters, and setting. • Evaluate your descriptions to make sure every word is pulling its weight.	• Rev up the conflict—you don't want your main character to skate right through your story. • Give your character a little taste of victory. (After all, you don't want him to give up too soon!)

13	14	15	16
• Enrich your sub-plots to keep your story interesting and readers on their toes. • Make sure your scenes are connected and in a logical order.	• Check out week's work for any potential plot holes that you'll have to address later. • Finish Act II, Part 1. **50% Completed!**	**Welcome to Week 3: Act II, Part 2** • Start thinking about your story's theme and how to weave it into your storyline.	• Evaluate the wholeness of each scene and each scene sequence of scenes.

17	18	19	20
• Set up your Act II turning point by crafting your reversal. • Keep an eye on your pacing.	• Make sure your story fits into the genre in which you're writing.	• Identify your best writing hours so that you'll know when to be at your desk. • Make your villain more complex—the big face-off is coming up.	• Complete your Act II turning point. • Check to make sure your hero is on the right path.

21	22	23	24
• Give your hero a reason to keep going. • Finish Act II, Part 2. **75% Completed!**	**Welcome to Week 4: Act III** • Identify your goal for this week—it's important for you to stay focused. • Make sure your villain is properly motivated.	• Take a look at how your main character is progressing.	• Develop final obstacle for your characters to overcome. • Craft a riveting climactic scene.

25	26	27	28
• Determine how to best reveal your theme. • Prepare for your story's resolution—remember, no loose ends.	• Verify that your story delivers on its promise to readers.	• Check your progress—you only have a few days to go.	• Do a final story check to identify areas that may need to be revised later.

29	30
• Start thinking about your next project.	• Finish Act III. • Rate your BIAM experience. • Celebrate! **100% Completed!**

Welcome to Week 1! One thing you should know before jumping into this BIAM: *This is going to be lots of fun.*

You have to start with a positive attitude. Are you positive about this experience? Get your mind positive about it now. The only thing we can control in life is how we react to events. You are embarking on the fulfillment of your dream. You will have a full manuscript in 30 days. How does that feel? Pretty darn good, right? Don't expect a perfect manuscript. Just expect words on pages.

If you really want to be negative, I'm sure you can easily find a reason to be negative. The truth is, being negative won't really get you anywhere in life. So make the decision to be positive, at least for 30 days, at least in regard to your BIAM. Can you do that? Be negative about other areas of your life if you want to, but don't allow that negativity to come into this BIAM process.

When you have a positive attitude you:

- believe in yourself ("I know I can complete my book in a month");

- see the best in every situation ("I didn't write much yesterday, but I will use one of my 'emergency days' to make up for it");

- focus on solutions to problems ("My Act II turning point isn't working ... the heroine needs to assert herself more in Act I to make the turning point believable"); and

- remain persistent ("Nothing will stop me from writing today, even if I have to write at midnight").

Keep this handy. Writers tend to have trouble seeing the best in their work, but drama and conflict are part of the trade. If you try to have a positive attitude, you will soon develop the above qualities. It is just a natural by-product of being positive.

> **The minute you feel some negativity rising, acknowledge it, experience it for a moment, and then let it go.**

Negativity can close us down and push our muses away. Writers cannot afford to be negative—literally! Of course, some writers are successful even though they are negative, but make no mistake about it: They are successful *in spite* of their negativity, not because of it. Why create another obstacle for yourself, anyway? The same goes for the tortured, alcoholic artist. Too many beginning writers have this image of the successful tortured, alcoholic writer and think, on some level, that a successful writer must be that way. Again, those writers were successful in spite of being tortured alcoholics, not because of it. So don't buy into those absurd romantic notions. Be *positive*. Make things easier on yourself.

This week, the focus is on Act I main plot points—from the setup to the first turning point.

TRADITIONAL STORY STRUCTURE: ACT I

The more you have absorbed traditional story structure, the easier it is not only to write without outlining too much ahead of time, but also to *break* those traditional rules. A quick review of traditional structure can help you a great deal when writing quickly. The more it is ingrained in your brain, the more you will write from instinct. You will automatically write toward the next plot point or act without even trying to.

Just as the acts themselves are guideposts when writing fast, other story elements, such as turning points, are small signs to help you stay on track between acts. When writing fast, you sometimes need to fall back on structure to help you make the right story decisions. There really is a reason for everything in BIAM.

Does following the basic three-act structure push you into writing a formulaic story? No; it is always the *execution* of the story that makes it so. Some stories do start out formulaically, but they evolve in the subsequent rewrites. Authors who write formulaic stories don't spend enough time rewriting and/or they don't spend enough time creating a detailed outline.

So, what is traditional story structure? Traditional story structure is the basic bare bones of a story and how it progresses. Traditional structure is not the only structure available to you, but it makes for a great basic structure from which you can jump into many creative interpretations. Know the rules first, then you can break them. For example, while you have a beginning, middle, and end in traditional story structure, you could be writing a film-noir type of hard-boiled detective story. This type of story would typically have the "ending" (a murder) in the opening chapter. From there, the entire story could be a flashback telling readers why the murder happened. So the structure or placement of events is moved around a bit—but there's still a clear beginning, middle, and end within it.

In the first of four short excerpts from my book *Story Structure Architect*, let's take a quick look at the crucial story components that come into play in Act I. We'll also look at how these story components play themselves out in the films *Casablanca* and *Dracula*, so that you can see how they're all interconnected.

As I said earlier, a traditional three-act story structure has a clear beginning, middle, and end. Act I is the setup, Act II is the development, and Act III is the climax and resolution. There is usually a turning point at the end of Act I and at the end of Act II to propel the story forward. The traditional Act I elements include:

• **The Setup:** The setup provides readers with the direction of the story. It gives all the information needed to get the story rolling, conveys the story genre, and establishes the pacing.

• **The Mood or Tone:** What about your story could convey mood or tone to readers? Is there a particular setting or character that encapsulates the feel of the story? Think about this for a moment: What if your story opened in a graveyard? Or a bank? Each location sets a different mood.

• **The Hook, Catalyst, or Inciting Incident:** This is a dynamic event that draws readers into the story. The main goal or problem may not be stated just yet, but something happens that piques interest. It can be an action (someone is murdered), a dialogue (a character receives a mysterious phone call), or a situation (a character is thrust into circumstances she may not be able to handle). This is the initial problem or situation that will become more complicated as the main goal or problem is introduced, which forces conflict.

CASABLANCA

The story opens with an image of a spinning globe and the sounds of "La Marseillaise," the French national anthem. A narrator explains the importance of the city of Casablanca as a place people would journey to in their escape from the Nazis during World War II. In Casablanca, they could search for an exit visa or letters of transit. Over a radio, we hear the French police announcing that two German officers were murdered on a train and that the train is headed for Casablanca. A German officer, Major Strasser, arrives at the Casablanca airport and is greeted by the local French Captain, Louis Renault. Strasser asks about the couriers, and Louis says that the murderer, like everyone else, will be at Rick's—a club owned by an American expatriate—tonight.

Jonathan Harker, a young clerk, journeys through the picturesque country-side of Transylvania on his way to meet with the mysterious Count Dracula regarding a real estate transaction. The beautiful scenery is interrupted by the superstition of the local people telling him not to venture into the castle. While he is frightened, he continues on, attacked by wolves on his way. He arrives at the castle to find a very hospitable Count, yet he feels he is somehow held captive.

• **The Serious Problem and/or Goal:** Why do we care? What is at stake? Don't be afraid to make things hard on your characters. You should always come up with several different problems to choose from. Who knows, you may even throw numerous problems at them at once. Think about the type of story you are writing and the genre you want to work in—what kinds of problems do characters usually have in these stories? How can you make your story different? This first serious problem or goal drives the story forward, so make it good. It motivates the main character and, when combined with the initial problem, adds that crucial first dose of conflict that's going to grow throughout the story. Each genre has its own type of expected problems and conflict:

• Romance: relationship conflict
• Horror: life and death conflict
• Drama: everyday problems intensified
• Comedy: everyday problems exaggerated
• Mystery: knowledge-related conflict

• **The Villain:** Who or what opposes the main character? Somehow, you need to introduce the villain. You can show him in a brief scene that conveys his villainous behavior, you can have other characters talk about him foreshadowing his arrival, or you can infer that something bad is coming but is, as of yet, unknown.

- **The Main Characters:** All of the main characters need to be introduced as soon as possible. It would be great to introduce all the supporting characters as well, but remember to keep your cast of characters to a bare minimum. It's very difficult to follow more than four main characters at a time. And please don't have all their names start with the same letter—Danny, Donald, and Damon can get confusing. You can combine several characters into one character, too. Instead of having a lawyer and a chiropractor, have a lawyer/chiropractor, or a lawyer who handles medical law.

Notice in the following examples how the initial problem is compounded by the introduction of the serious one; together, the two of these form the major conflict for your character or characters in the story.

CASABLANCA

The letters of transit that the German officers were carrying wind up at Rick's, and Rick is asked to hide them. He agrees, but that is not the only 'serious problem,' as Rick's long-lost love, Ilsa, walks into the café with her husband, Laszlo, in search of letters of transit to escape the Nazis. The villains are not only the Nazis and the police, but also Laszlo, the husband.

DRACULA

Harker realizes the Count has supernatural powers and begins to fear for his life when a brief glimpse at a photo of Harker's fiancée, Mina, evokes a strong, strange reaction from the Count (who believes Mina to be his lost love reincarnated). When the Count leaves his castle in pursuit of Mina, Harker tries to escape, fending off the Count's evil vampire women in the process.

• **The Turning Point:** A turning point is like a cliffhanger, or a moment where the story is taken in a new direction and we wonder what will happen next. A turning point may accomplish a variety of functions, such as pushing the story in a new direction or asking questions that make us wonder about the outcome of the story.

• **Theme:** A theme is a recurring motif usually provoked by the turning point question. As the central question or conflict is presented again and again throughout the course of the story, and as the stakes are continually raised, how the character responds will determine the overall theme for the story. You don't need to identify or make your theme concrete at this point, but you will inevitably find yourself writing toward it from the very beginning. (We'll be discussing theme more in depth in Week 3.)

CASABLANCA

Rick, who is shown in the setup as a tough, fiercely independent man out only for himself, is shaken by the appearance of Ilsa, his true, lost love. In a scene where Ilsa tries to confront Rick, the formerly confident, assured man is shown drunk, angry, and out of control. "Of all the gin joints in all the towns in all the world," Rick says, "she walks into mine." Thus, the turning point of the story comes from the conflict, the merging of the initial and serious problems, and how Rick deals with it: He can help Ilsa and Laszlo escape, thereby losing her forever, or he can try to hold on, putting her, Laszlo, and himself in grave danger. How his character changes (or doesn't) to handle this conflict will develop and reveal theme.

DRACULA

Harker's association with the Count has put not only himself, but also his bride-to-be, Mina, at risk. The ship the Count was traveling on shows up near Mina's residence with all the crew dead. We also know it will take Harker a long time to reach home. Mina and her young friend Lucy are in danger now. The two problems from the setup have thus merged, and the major conflict/turning point of the story—the Count's pursuit of Mina and Harker's need to save her—is in place. Also, a number of themes—among them the permanence or transience of love, not to mention life—have presented themselves, but how they will play out remains to be seen.

DAY 1

Your work is to discover your work, and then, with all your heart, to give yourself to it.

—BUDDHA

OBJECTIVES

• Write a one-sentence summary that will act as the spine of your story, or as a reference point as you outline and write the first draft.

• Complete the Story Idea Map worksheet, which will help you to start brainstorming more ideas for your story.

WRITE A ONE-SENTENCE SUMMARY

So what's the one-liner for your story? Can you tell me, in one sentence, what your story is about? This is tough, I know, but give it a try. Just include the very basic elements of your story idea, the overall story in a nutshell. Don't include the plot points or acts, just create a tagline of sorts to tell readers what your story is about. What would publishers put on the back of the book to let readers know what your story is about? What would you envision on a film poster for your story? Go to the local movie theater or rental store to read some posters if you need to. They always have great taglines to promote a film.

If you took everything away—the plot points, subplots, settings, etc.—what is the core storyline that is left? For instance:

• A rich girl and poor boy meet and fall in love on the ill-fated voyage of the Titanic.

- A Hobbit named Frodo, entrusted with an ancient ring, must now embark on an epic quest to destroy it.

ONE-SENTENCE STORY SUMMARY

The point of this exercise is that, if you can't tell me in one line what the core of your story is, then you may not have much to focus on while writing. You can't get from A to Z, especially in 30 days, without some kind of map. Even those of you who hate to outline must do this little exercise. You have to have some kind of direction, even if that direction is a broad one.

This is your one-sentence outline. It is what all other elements of your outline will be held up to. For instance, you might find yourself wondering, "Should I include this specific scene in the detailed outline?" You can find the answer to this question by asking yourself, "Does it fit with my one-sentence outline?"

For example, in *Titanic*, you want to add a scene where Rose learns to play the harmonica in her room because you just love the harmonica. Does the scene really have anything to do with the love story (the story's core idea)? Does it have anything to do with how poorly the ship is made or that it will eventually sink (the plot's core idea)? Does it do anything to advance the core story? Not really. Unless you can make it fit with the core story and advance it somehow, drop it. If Jack teaches her how to play it and the sharing of the harmonica adds some romantic tension (perhaps her fiancé or mother walks in), then maybe it will fit.

The one-sentence summary is similar to a thesis statement in non-fiction. All the ideas you have are held up to it to see if they fit with the story. This way, you don't go off on tangents, spinning your wheels in the wrong direction—oh, what a writing block that is!

MAP YOUR STORY IDEAS

Start brainstorming some ideas for your Act I arc using the following Story Idea Map. This worksheet outlines the basic Act I structure, using your setup to develop the basic plot situations or problems into conflict (where Act II will begin).

Don't censor yourself; just jot down any ideas that come to mind. List any potential characters, both major and minor, as they occur to you—perhaps there will be characters you would expect to find in this kind of story; perhaps you'll be surprised by unusual or atypical characters (possibly used to further comedic or dramatic effect, depending on your goals). If you get an idea for a setting, prop, secondary character, what-have-you, write it down and keep brainstorming. Don't be afraid to twist an idea around and create an outrageous Act I.

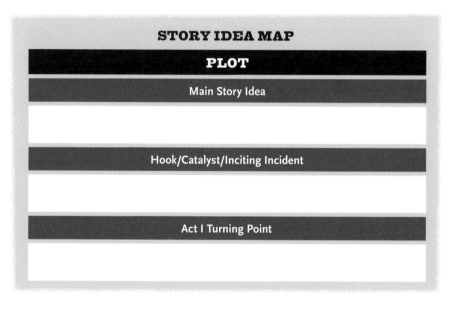

STORY IDEA MAP

PLOT

Main Story Idea

Hook/Catalyst/Inciting Incident

Act I Turning Point

The Stakes

CHARACTERS

Major Characters	Minor Characters

SETTING

Setting	Props

DAY 2

Seize the day, and put the least possible trust in tomorrow.

—HORACE

OBJECTIVES

• Fill out your ten scene cards so you will have a basic idea of your story and the direction it is going in.

• Hone your scenes. Remember that having fewer scenes can actually make a good story even better.

When I worked as a film analyst, I noticed that A-level movies had approximately ten to twenty scenes total, and B-level movies had thirty-five to sixty scenes total. This happened in every single case. Some A-level movies are now three hours long, but even so, the better movies just don't have as many scenes as the lesser ones do. The writers of the B movies were trying to do too much, switching scenes to try and make it seem as if there were a lot of action or drama taking place. They didn't use the scenes they had to full effect. They didn't use the opportunities for action and drama that were right in front of them.

Everyone knows (hopefully) about the film *Jaws*. There is a scene where the three men sit on the boat waiting for the shark to show up. They drink, talk, reveal things about their histories and characters. It is a wonderful scene that advances the plot, reveals character, and entertains the audience all at the same time. If this movie were written by a B-movie writer, I can surmise that this one great scene would have been chopped up into several short scenes in different locations, never standing still long enough to develop the characters and the plot.

How does this translate to writing if you are working on a novel and not a screenplay? If it helps you, think of it as events instead of scenes. So, you guessed it, I want you to develop your story's ten key scenes—think opening scene, turning point scenes, climactic scene, etc. Your final outline may contain more scenes, especially if you are writing an epic piece or if your genre calls for it, but just try to come up with your story's ten core scenes in the order they will appear. If you were to pitch your story to an editor, what ten key scenes would you illustrate? (These scenes are also going to be the longest and most detailed in the story.) You can use index cards if you like, but I have provided ten boxes in the appendix, so you can keep all your notes for this story within the pages of this book.

I am not talking about ten *chapters* here; I am talking about ten *scenes*. You may have one scene in a diner that takes up several chapters of a novel, as you switch from one character's point of view to the next, but all these chapters are focused on the same scene. Or you may have a big event that takes several chapters and uses several locations. You may stop a scene temporarily to start a new chapter to tell readers what another character outside of this scene is doing, but when you come back to it, you are still working on that one scene.

Now, don't get confused—I am not talking about *location* here, either. Think about this: Many low-budget filmmakers have to save money by shooting films that take place in one location. Now, they still had numerous scenes in that one location (*Reservoir Dogs, Four Rooms, The Telephone,* and *Live Nude Girls* are examples of this). They have all their scenes taking place in one location. Scenes are not about locations. They are the beginning, middle, and end of a small piece of your story.

You know the first scene will be an *introduction* of the story and the last scene will be the *ending*, so take your time and figure out what the other eight scenes are. Once you do this, you can see if you need to add more scenes. You can even jot down how many pages you think each scene will take. Then look over each of the ten scenes, before you add any additional scenes, and see if you are using the full potential of each scene by answering the following questions:

- **Can you reveal more about the characters?** In the *Jaws* example, you see firsthand the different personalities and eccentricities of each character; they are stuck in the same place, after all, and can't get away from each other. You also see how each personality fits in with the others.

- **Does it advance the plot at all?** In *Jaws*, the shark shows up and pushes things forward (literally), and we get a feel for how this whole thing will end. We believe the actions of the old captain in the end because we just learned so much about his behavior here.

- **What can you add to this scene to make it more interesting, so you don't feel the need to switch to another scene right away?** In *Jaws*, the writer could have had them wait for the shark a bit and then move on. Instead, we stop for some wonderful characterization and dialogue. The anticipation of waiting for the shark is always there.

- **Are you using enough props, subtext, and dialogue?** In the *Jaws* example, they play around with rope, drink, show off their scars. We have a whole range of emotions going on, including humor—"I think we need a bigger boat" is a classic line in the film.

DRAFT YOUR SCENE CARDS

On pages 236 through 245 of the appendix, you'll find ten guided scene cards (I've included a sample one for you here). Think about how your story should progress, and jot down details as they come to you, revising as you go along. You will probably come back to these cards to flesh them out a bit more as you write. You may want to use a pencil so you can erase ideas as needed. The cards are small enough so you won't go overboard and write too much, which can leave no room for creativity as you write the story later as well. You might consider how the earlier *Jaws* example fits into this scene structure; nevertheless, the arc of your story is *yours* to construct, so you'll want to consider carefully what your major scenes or narrative points might be and where you feel they naturally fit into your overall story. (For a more detailed outline of overall structure, see Day 3.)

I just want you to think of your story in terms of ten key scenes. This really will help you focus your idea so you can pepper the story with the more important details later. Think about this way: If you only had to write one scene and had three days to do it, how wonderful would that scene be? Probably your best one ever!

So what if you only had ten key scenes and twenty days to write them? They would probably be pretty good too! (The remaining ten days go the other, less important filler scenes.)

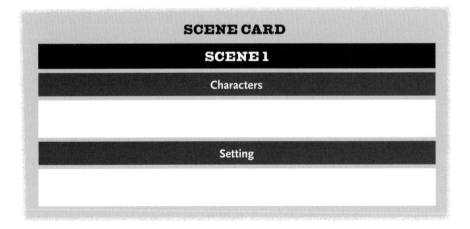

Mood/Tone

Scene Objective

DAY 3

The only limits to our realizations of tomorrow will be our doubts of today.

—FRANKLIN D. ROOSEVELT

OBJECTIVES

- Draft an At-A-Glance Outline using your ten scenes to help you start writing.

- Develop a more detailed outline on your own using the At-A-Glance Outline if you want to.

- Start keeping notes on what you need to research so that when you have the time, you know where to focus your efforts.

- If you haven't started writing yet—start!

You should be writing every day now. These exercises don't take that much time, and you can use them to jump-start the creative process and then dive into your draft. It is actually easier to fill out the worksheets after you have started writing a bit. You have more of a feel for what you want to say.

COMPLETE YOUR AT-A-GLANCE OUTLINE

I know many of you don't like to outline, which is fine. I have written without an outline myself in the past, though I'd have to admit the outline probably was in my head already.

When attempting a BIAM, it is critical to have, at the very least, a solid direction to go in. There just isn't as much time to "go with the flow" and wait to see what comes up. Things will come up and you can go with them, but you have to give yourself a road to travel down in the first place. Remember: It is much easier and faster to rewrite an outline than to rewrite an entire manuscript.

You don't have to have a detailed outline with every scene mapped out (though that would be great!), but at least know the direction you want to go in, the gist of the main characters—will they succeed or fail in the end?

This outline offers a quick way to fill in the blanks of your story. It guides you to answer the right questions for each area of your story, the questions that will come up when writing fast. It forces you to think about some of the important details like, "What type of props would be found in the setting I chose?" The answer to this may then spark an idea when you are writing:

> I could have the villain use a shredder to hide evidence of his indiscretions, since he will be in an office building during this scene.

Or:

> I want to get really creative here ... I could move this whole scene to the zoo and have a goat eat the receipts showing he was out with another woman ...

This At-A-Glance Outline will cover all three acts and be a guide throughout your 30-day BIAM. I know many of you don't like to outline, but I'd like you to have some idea of where you are going, especially when you are writing fast. Remember: Writing without a plot usually means being okay with heavy rewriting.

Now let's fill out the At-A-Glance Outline. There are a lot of details to consider at this stage. Don't panic if you don't know how all of your story's pieces fit together yet—sometimes different elements of your story reveal themselves to you as you write. Right now, just fill out what you can. If a part of the outline stumps you, don't get frustrated. Just think it over. Brainstorm some possibilities and try to fill it in as best you can, because this outline will act as your BIAM road map. If you're still stuck, leave that box blank. Don't stop the whole process because you can't answer one question. Keep moving forward and do your best.

AT-A-GLANCE OUTLINE

TITLE

ACT I (WEEK 1)

Briefly describe what happens in Act I from the initial story hook to the turning point.

Describe the setup.

Describe how the mood or tone is created (props, weather, emotions, setting, characters, style).

Identify the hook/incident.

Identify the first turning point.

Identify what is at stake (why readers should care).

Protagonist's Introduction	Protagonist's Motivation	Details to Remember

Antagonist's Introduction	Antagonist's Motivation	Details to Remember

Supporting Character 1	Supporting Character 2	Unusual Supporting Character

Setting	Props	Time Period

ACT II, PART 1 (WEEK 2)

Briefly describe what happens in the first half of Act II, from where the problem intensifies to the temporary triumph.

Describe how you want readers to feel (mood/tone) when reading this act. Also think about how you want the protagonist to feel.

Describe how the problem intensifies.

Describe the temporary triumph. Is it an inner (psychological) and/or external triumph for the protagonist?

Think about how this triumph can be foreshadowed.

Decide whether a subplot plays a role or causes any effect.

Main Setting for Act II	Other Settings	Props

Any New Characters	Why They Are Needed	Things to Remember

ACT II, PART 2 (WEEK 3)

Briefly describe what happens in the second half of Act II, from the reversal to the second turning point.

Describe how you want readers to feel (mood/tone) when reading this act. Also think about how you want the protagonist to feel.

Describe how you will create and show the reversal.

Describe the second turning point. Think about how it relates to or sets up the final resolution in Act III.

Think about how you can foreshadowed the second turning point in Act I or in the first half of Act II.

Describe how the hero's decisions cause this turning point.

Setting for Second Turning Point	Other Settings Used	Props
New Characters	**Why They Are Needed**	**Things to Remember**

ACT III (WEEK 4)

Briefly describe what happens in Act III, from the final obstacle to the resolution.

Describe the final obstacle.

Describe how the mood or tone is created (props, weather, emotions, setting, characters, style).

Describe the climax.

Note any loose ends you might need to tie up in the resolution.

Describe how you want readers to feel when they finish the story.

Think about whether your villain is defeated in the end. If he is, how? What are his crucial mistakes? How are readers likely to respond to his failure or success?

Think about whether your hero wins in the end. If he does, how? What does he learn through his victory or defeat? What is his biggest accomplishment or mistake?

Describe your story's theme.

Congratulations! You have just completed your At-A-Glance Outline.

For those of you who wish to write more detailed notes for yourself, feel free to do so. Just don't let yourself get sidetracked. It's time to jump in and start writing! I know many of you will just move forward with the At-A-Glance Outline, and that is okay.

START YOUR RESEARCH

Use the following Research Tracker worksheet to write down areas you notice that are going to need to be researched later on—from setting props and location details to character slang and weaponry. Anything that needs to be looked up, double-checked, referenced, or further developed can be indicated here. Jot it down and keep writing. Later, when you have the time and enough things to research, you can sit down and do it all at once. This saves a lot of time and gets things out of your head. For instance:

Topic to Research	What to Look for	Findings
Guns in 1929	Caliber? Safety?	45, 50, & 51 (50 had controllability and follow-up speed problems)

This is your research sheet for the entire 30-day BIAM process. Do what you can, when you can. Research a little one day, wait several days if needed, and then come back to it again. It is much easier (and less time consuming) if you research several things at once. In the end, though, it is up to you when you do the research. Every project will be different, so there are no set days for researching.

RESEARCH TRACKER

Topic to Research	What to Look for	Findings

DAY 4

The Mighty Oak was once a little nut that held its ground.

—Anonymous

OBJECTIVES

- Create a Character Story Sketch to help you remember little details about all of your characters.

- Create Character Snapshots for your main characters that help you to add depth to them.

- Think through your Character-Revealing Scenes in order to have interesting scenes ready that you know will reveal deeper aspects of your characters.

DEVELOP YOUR CHARACTERS

While the BIAM 30-day plan is all about getting down the plot (that's why we do the plot outline first), characterization is still extremely important. It doesn't matter if you are writing a character-driven story or a plot-driven one; the plot is still what you are focusing on when writing quickly. Character-driven pieces just have the characters driving the plot forward.

Many writers like to map out their characters before they start writing, while others like to wait until they have written a little of the story and gotten to meet their characters before mapping them out. The following worksheets represent a middle ground of sorts—allowing you to think through certain aspects without going too deep too early in the writing process. What I have created here are three distinct worksheets that will help you get to know your characters better *and* help you plan for and chart their growth throughout your story:

- **Character Story Sketch:** This worksheet helps to bring out those elements that relate to the plot as well as the standard biographical elements. For example: "Sara is a tall brunette with a few extra pounds and whole lot of confidence."

- **Character Snapshot:** This worksheet provides a quick overview of your main characters and expands on the story sketch information, revealing more depth about the psychology of each character. Under "Trauma," for instance, you might write: "Sara was abused as a child."

- **Character-Revealing Scenes:** This worksheet allows you to outline the possible scenes that will reveal each of the categories in the Character Story Sketch and Character Snapshot worksheets regarding the main characters. (You can use the scenes you have listed in your outline if you want to and add elements to reveal the main characters.) For example, a scene that relates to the character's "Trauma" might be: "Sara watches as the woman in the store hits her daughter. Her muscles tighten. She just can't contain herself, not after what she went through as a child. No. She has to speak up!"

Do you see how this works? Create a Character Story Sketch to get a handle on the basics of who a character is. Use that information to go a little deeper and come up with a more precise Character Snapshot. Then use the information from your Character Snapshot to complete the Character-Revealing Scenes worksheet by taking each topic area from the snapshot to come up with different scenes to reveal this information. In each box, write a possible scene you could have to reveal the main character. You don't have to use these scenes, but if and when you get stuck, you will have some great scenes to fall back on.

Let's say that as you brainstorm for the "Psychology/Trauma" section of the Character Snapshot, you decide your heroine was attacked by a dog as a kid. When you get to the Character-Revealing Scenes worksheet, you can choose to write in the "Scenes to Reveal Trauma" section:

> When the heroine tries to confront the villain in Act II, a large dog wanders into her view and she freezes in silent panic, giving the villain a chance to escape.

Now, isn't that a much better way to "give the villain a chance to escape" than just arbitrarily having the villain escape by some other means? This way, you have come up with something that also reveals a bit about the heroine in the process. How do you think she will feel after he gets away now? Much worse than if she really tried to stop him and he got away without any real fault or failure of her own.

Or you could write in the "Scenes to Reveal Trauma" section:

> If needed, the heroine could be forced to confront several guard dogs to fulfill her objective or achieve a secondary goal.

If you find you need something to keep the story moving forward, you can look at the Character-Revealing Scenes worksheet and decide to add a guard dog to the scene and spice it up a bit.

Think about Harrison Ford as Indiana Jones and how his character can't stand snakes. It really adds a lot to several scenes when he must do something to save someone's life while confronting his fear of snakes at the same time. It also helps make his character feel more human.

CHARACTER STORY SKETCH

STORY TITLE	CHARACTER NAME

Age	Ethnicity	Height	Weight	Hair	Eyes

Education	Residence	Job	Archetype	Birth Sign	Religion

Style of Dress	
Distinguishing Marks	

FAVORITE THINGS

Music	Food	Color	Pastime	Entertainment

JUST THE FACTS

Children	
Pets	
Hobbies	

Family Secrets	
Worst Fear	
Greatest Hope	
Skills	
Prized Possession	
Vulnerability	
Regrets	
General Outlook	

GOING DEEPER

Describe the first impression this character makes.

Describe how and why other characters view this character.

Describe what this character needs to learn by the end of the story.

Describe how you will foreshadow this ending in the story's beginning.

CHARACTER SNAPSHOT

VITAL STATISTICS

Name

Nationality

Age

Family Situation

Appearance

Quirks

PSYCHOLOGY

Traumas

Feelings About Settings

Overall Attitude

Fears

Joys

ACCOMPLISHMENTS

Skills

Weaknesses

Awards/Degrees

Dreams/Ambitions

MOTIVATIONS

Top Priorities

Favorite Things/People

Obsessions

Guilts

CHARACTER ARC

Lessons to Learn

Intended Character Changes

IMPORTANT NOTES TO REMEMBER

Note: Remember that you have in your story not just a protagonist, whose goal is shaped or informed by who he is and where he's been, but you have an *an*tagonist, whose goal is in conflict with that of your main character. At the moment, having a clear understanding of what your villain's goal is will be enough to keep your story moving in the right direction. But as you write, you'll come to understand more of who your villain is and what parts of his own life have pushed him toward this goal. Rather than trying to map out the villain's upbringing, likes and dislikes, or personal tragedies now, taking up valuable writing time, keep a blank character sheet handy and make notes to yourself as more of your villain is revealed to you. (We'll refine our discussion on villains more in Weeks 3 and 4.)

CHARACTER-REVEALING SCENES

Scenes to reveal appearance:	Scenes to reveal quirks:
Scenes to reveal character's lesson:	**Revealing scenes for:**	**Scenes to reveal skills/ weaknesses:**
Scenes to reveal motivation:	Scenes to reveal trauma:

DAY 5

OBJECTIVE

- Hone the Act I turning point you created in your At-A-Glance Outline in order to make sure you have your readers hooked into this story and have the raw material to set up your Act II turning point, which propels us into the final climax in Act III.

DEVELOP YOUR ACT I TURNING POINT

You should be well on your way to reaching the end of Act I—the turning point. In novels, this means getting the first 25 percent or so of the book completed.

A turning point is basically an event or new information that turns the story in a new direction, for the readers or for the character (sometimes readers know what will happen but the character doesn't). The best turning points are the ones where readers have no idea it is coming. On one page readers think things will go on one way, then the next page (turning point) everything changes, and the readers are excited about the possibilities. For example:

> The heroine meets the love of her life, and readers expect the story to progress along, leading to a marriage at the end. Readers are enjoying the story, but not expecting too much, when all of a sudden the heroine sees the hero with another woman but can't be sure about what is going on. Now what

the readers assumed was going to happen may not happen; something is at stake here.

Or:

The heroine meets the love of her life ... then she gets news she has only six months to live.

Or:

The heroine meets the love of her life ... but he has a secret life.

Or:

The heroine meets the love of her life ... then she walks out of her office building and finds someone shooting at her.

Things have been turned around in a new direction! Look back at your outline from Day 3 and state your Act I turning point here:

ACT I TURNING POINT

Brainstorm a bit using the following worksheet to see if there are any other ideas you can use, any other directions you can go in, or different character reactions to this turning point that could spice things up. Play with your turning point to see if it brings up any possibilities.

ACT I TURNING POINT BRAINSTORM

What is the exact opposite that could happen at this turning point?

What is the most outrageous thing that could happen at this point?

What would happen if you brought in another character?

How do you want readers to react or feel at this point?

DAY 6

You can't wait for inspiration. You have to go after it with a club.

—Jack London

OBJECTIVES

• Use your At-A-Glance Outline, character sheets, and Act I Turning Point Brainstorm to spend the day fleshing out Act I.

• Fill out the Backstory Brainstorm worksheet so you know how much backstory to include in your opening.

KEEP WRITING

Don't lose steam now. Getting to the end of the first week will motivate you to keep going. Yes, Act II may look daunting, but if writing were easy, everyone would do it. This is where dedication and discipline come into play. Look at that signed book contract. Keep your word to yourself. This is only 30 days, after all. The second half of Week 1 is specifically designed to be a bit light so you can really jump into the story and get going.

BALANCE YOUR BACKSTORY

Backstory is crucial to adding richness and depth to a story. It helps readers better understand a character and/or situation, as it is directly related to the story's main problem and is usually the source of a main character's flaws. Take a look back at your Day 3 At-A-Glance Outline. You might find that you touched on crucial backstory elements in several sections, especially in those related to setup and character motivation. Your Day 4 character worksheets also should provide you with some insight into the story's backstory. Now, not all of this potential backstory is going to make it into your story—some of it will, and some of it will simply inform or color what you write without you ever having to mention it directly.

In the following Backstory Brainstorm worksheet, determine which nuggets of backstory are just for you—the writer—and which ones actually belong in your story. Next, make sure the details you choose to include are relevant to the frontstory (if they're not, then think about whether you really need to include them). After that, think about where this information would fit best. Perhaps you want to reveal your main character's backstory slowly, dropping only a small clue in the opening scene. Or maybe you're planning a big flashback scene near the end of Act I that's going to foreshadow events in Act II. Whatever you decide, just make sure that your backstory has a direct tie to your frontstory and that you don't overload your opening scene and bog down your readers with too many details that won't mean anything to them yet (we'll discuss balancing out your opening scene next).

BACKSTORY BRAINSTORM

Backstory for Me	Backstory to Include	Relevance to Frontstory	Possible Scene Locations

If you've already completed your opening scene, it's important to make sure you haven't explained too much. Most editors say writers tend to go into unnecessary backstory before finally getting the story rolling in chapter two. Take a look at your opening scene, and consider the following questions:

- Is it action oriented?
- Do you have a lot of explanation?
- Do you leave readers wondering what the heck is going on?

The best way to figure out if you've overdone it with the backstory is to go through your opening chapter and highlight in yellow all your descriptive words and action-related passages where the character acts, reacts, or makes a decision.

Then go through your opening chapter again and highlight in pink all passages that convey backstory information. These passages may explain what is going on, what happened in the past, or why things are as they are.

What do you notice?

If you have a lot of pink highlighting, then you have way too much backstory going on. Find some backstory passages that really don't need to be there right now, jot them on your notes sheet, and delete them. Then later on, while you are working on Act II, perhaps, you can work that information into the story in a more interesting way.

If you have a lot of yellow highlighting, then you either have just enough backstory or perhaps too little. The best way to figure this out is to have someone else you *trust* read just the opening chapter to see if she understands the story. If she does, then you are probably right on track here.

It is a tricky thing, I know, but now you have a system to help you figure this out. You can also watch film versions of your favorite books to see how they cut back on the backstory and start in the action. All films do this, so it can be a great way to learn how to work with backstory.

Ultimately, it is your call. Editors like it when you start the story early, but they also like to know what is going on. Find a balance between the two.

DAY 7

My life has been filled with terrible misfortune, most of which never happened.
—MICHEL DE MONTAIGNE

OBJECTIVE

- Complete the Plot Hole Checklist and the Character Hole Checklist so you can see right away if there are any problems with your story.

FIND AND FILL STORY HOLES

Now is the time to start finding all the holes in your story. You don't want to write one hundred pages only to have a friend say, "Why would they do that?" or "The whole premise just doesn't seem logical."

Think about the questions on the following checklist as you review your draft thus far. This does not mean you should go back and rewrite if you find holes. Just use your notes sheet and keep writing.

PLOT HOLE CHECKLIST

☐ Does everything in the idea/summary make sense?
☐ Are the characters motivated?
☐ Will the readers suspend disbelief?
☐ Will the characters act as they are expected to? If not, did you set up why they won't?
☐ Is the story's world set up properly?
☐ Is it clear why the antagonist is doing what he is doing?
☐ Is it clear why the protagonist cares about the goal?
☐ Does the protagonist come into contact/conflict with the antagonist in a manner that is organic to the story?

□ Do all the characters have a purpose, a reason for being there?
□ Are all the setting props organic to the setting?
□ Is the goal feasible?

Traditional stories won't have as many holes as the more challenging, unusual stories will, but even so, take a moment to see that your outline and the writing you've done thus far make sense. In other words, make sure your story has *verisimilitude*, a sense of plausible, consistent, and believable reality.

For instance, if you have three elderly characters escape from a nursing home in the U.S. to run off to Egypt, let the readers know how this came about. It isn't normal for this to happen, certainly, and having them decide go on a whim isn't believable; otherwise, why wouldn't they have gone the day before? A week before? What is it that motivates this particular action now? They need some major motivation and opportunity for this to happen, which requires plausibility and consistency on your part in both motivation and the way the action is pursued. They need passports, after all; otherwise, come up with a way that they don't need passports. (Does one of them have a wealthy son who owns a private plane? Did another fly in the war? Is the parent of the wealthy son just perturbed enough over being in a home to "borrow" the plane?)

Writers of more fantastic or far-out stories must pay *particular* attention to verisimilitude, as the rules that govern "real life" aren't necessarily those that govern your story. For example, if one dog in the story is able to talk when no other dogs can talk, you should explain how this happened. Ask yourself: "Will readers just buy this, or will they question it?" If every animal in the story can talk, then readers will just accept it, because you have created a world where all dogs talk. But, if only one dog can talk, that world hasn't been created and readers need to know what is going on. In a science fiction story, perhaps the dog was part of an experiment. In a fantasy or magical realist story, perhaps readers accept the reality of the situation because the characters in the story do: "Fido was a dog with excellent vocabulary but poor pronunciation." Remember, the reader will allow you to set the rules of your world as long as those rules remain consistent; no one likes the rules to change in the middle of the game.

Every writer, not just the fantasy writer, must keep verisimilitude in mind; any out-of-place detail can destroy the "reality" of your story. Say your heroine is out in the country, in the middle of nowhere, and the villain comes along and attacks her. She stumbles over a fire hydrant, turns it on, and knocks the villain down from the water pressure. Where did that fire hydrant come from? It is not organic, and the readers need some sort of explanation. (Perhaps there is a house hidden nearby.)

These are the things to look for. Once you find a problem, decide if you really need that element in the story and then brainstorm ways to explain it. You're making this world from the ground up, after all; make sure it sets and follows the rules you need it to.

CHARACTER HOLE CHECKLIST

☐ Have you set up and built all the major characters?

☐ Do you introduce the protagonist and antagonist in a way that makes a strong first impression on readers.

☐ Do you announce the story goal (or at least hint at it)?

☐ Does everything make sense to the readers?

☐ Do the main characters act "in character"? If not, why?

☐ Have you hinted at some of the issues uncovered in the Character Snapshot worksheet?

☐ Have you used any of your revealing scenes? If not, can you tweak a scene to add one?

☐ Are all actions motivated?

☐ Do the characters react to the turning point in a believable manner?

Come up with your own questions to ponder, as well, and make notes of these things on your worksheets. Don't go back and rewrite just yet, even if you finish Act I early. Keep moving forward and get a jump on Act II if you want to, but don't stop to rewrite. You are just making notes of holes to fix when you rewrite. By the time you get to the end, you will forget a lot of Act I issues, and you don't need to take up valuable "creative mental space" with such information.

WEEK 1 WRAP-UP

Congratulations! This is the end of the first week. As you close out this week and prepare for Week 2, consider the following:

- Did you get that outline finished or at least have a direction to go in (for you non-plotters)?

- Do you have areas you need to research?

- Did you set up all the main characters?

- Did you define the protagonist's goal(s)?

- Do you have an interesting setting?

- Do you have an incident, plot twist, or character reveal for the ending of Act I?

PROGRESS TRACKER

Week 1: 25%	Week 2: 50%	Week 3: 75%	Week 4: 100%
███████			

Welcome to Week 2! Congratulations on finishing Week 1 and sticking around. This week will focus on the first half of Act II—intensifying the problem and getting to the temporary triumph. This is flexible and meant only as a guidepost to keep you on track. BIAM doesn't force you to do anything; we just use the most common language (traditional story structure) so we can all be on the same page.

In the end, it doesn't matter how much you wrote last week as long as you stuck with it and gave it your all. You are still here, which means you are showing that critical part of yourself that your book matters. Your dreams are important, and you will make time for them.

If nothing else, you are building a great habit here—sitting down to write every day. This is very important. Perhaps it will take you three BIAMs before you can be disciplined enough to write a full draft in 30 days, but just think: Each time, it's getting easier and easier. You are getting used to writing as a part of your lifestyle. You just have to focus more on the opening chapters and deal with any inner resistance you may have to accomplishing your dream. It's like dieting; if there weren't any inner resistance, everyone would go on one diet and be thin right away. We know it takes both inner and outer work. The fact that you finished Week 1 and are here for Week 2 is *huge*. Don't underestimate this accomplishment.

Week 2 is a critical week. During Week 1, you have all these possibilities in front of you, but as the week wears on, you can easily fall into negative thinking and give up, worried that you still have three more weeks looming in front of you. But once you get past Week 2, you are halfway there; you only have to repeat what you just accomplished. You'll have proven that you can write for two weeks at this level; then, you just have to do it again. Push yourself to get through Week 2. And remember to stay *positive.*

TRADITIONAL STORY STRUCTURE: ACT II, PART 1

In Act I, we established the basics of our story, introduced our main characters and set the book's tone, provided our protagonist with an initial problem to contend with, and then complicated things by adding a secondary serious problem. It is this serious problem, and how it informs or complicates the initial one, that creates the central conflict of the story for our protagonist and leads to our book's first crucial turning point ... leading us to Act II. How will the protagonist react to the conflict he's been presented with? Is he up to the challenge? Will things get worse before they get better? (Readers ask this question even knowing the answer: Yes, things are bound to.) The question for us, as writers, becomes one of how to navigate the protagonist through the difficult waters ahead—while making those waters a little deeper, a little riskier, as we go—to create a compelling and dynamic second act.

• **The Problem Intensifies:** There are three possible ways in which the problem can intensify here: barriers, complications, and situations.

> • **Barriers** occur when the character tries something and it doesn't work. The character must change directions or try another approach. (For example, the heroine tries to talk to get into the church to stop the wedding but the doors are locked, and several goons were told to watch for her and keep her out.)

> • **Complications** are action points that don't pay off immediately. Something new is introduced, be it a character or problem, that makes the current problem even worse than it already seems. (For example, an ex-girlfriend comes in when the hero is about to tell the heroine why he stood her up the other night; now the heroine's imagination is really in overdrive.)

> • **Situations** are when a new dramatic circumstances or predicaments happen to a character to move the story forward and add

tension. The story may take a bit of a detour as the entire begin-ning, middle, and end of a new situation or incident plays out; or the situation can be played out in pieces throughout the second act. (For example, the main character finds out his sister was arrested for narcotics and now his entire political campaign is in jeopardy.)

CASABLANCA

Rick has to deal with a series of complications—continuing pressure from Louis, who is on the one hand a friend (or something like it) and the other, by the nature of his job, an officer assisting the German investigation; from the Nazis, who are suspicious of Rick; and from Laszlo, who wants to purchase the visas Rick has in his possession. These complications are political in nature, illustrating the volatile cli-mate of Casablanca during the war, but they also serve to heighten the tension Rick faces over his personal complication: the fact that Ilsa and her husband need the stolen visas to leave Casablanca safely.

DRACULA

The Count creates many of his own barriers and complications. Attack-ing Lucy only brings him unwanted attention, and when Dr. Van Helsing is brought in to discover what strange malady Lucy is afflicted with, he figures out what is going on and takes action. The Count's need to sleep in soil from his homeland and avoid sunlight also works against him.

- **Temporary Triumph:** The main character thinks she has achieved her goal, but this triumph is short-lived. A reversal is just around the corner.

CASABLANCA

Ilsa visits Rick in his apartment and tells him she really does love him and wants to be with him. She answers all his questions about why she'd previously abandoned him in Paris, and they embrace. But Ilsa's professed feelings for Rick will only complicate things further; she still needs the letters so that Laszlo might escape, perhaps taking her along with him. The "victory" is, at best, bittersweet.

DRACULA

Lucy is attacked and killed by a wolf that storms her room—but Dr. Van Helsing, having seen the bite marks on her neck, realizes that she is not truly dead but undead and convinces Lucy's would-be suitors to accompany him to her crypt, where they find the formerly vivacious young woman transformed into a creature of the night. In order to save her, Van Helsing cuts off her head and stuffs her mouth with garlic, thereby reuniting her soul with God (if this isn't exactly a textbook temporary triumph, it seems in the neighborhood). Meanwhile, Harker is reunited with Mina, thanks to the assistance of a kindly convent that takes him in. Harker and Mina are married, though readers sense this "triumphant" moment is merely the calm before the storm.

DAY 8

All our dreams can come true, if we have the courage to pursue them.
—WALT DISNEY

OBJECTIVES

- Catch-up day! Finish anything you haven't completed from last week, and rework any worksheet you feel you need to revisit.

- Take some time to conduct a bit of research if needed.

- Reinforce your dedication and focus by making sure you stay solution-oriented as you continue the BIAM process.

Repeat the following affirmation to yourself every morning during Week 2 and see what happens:

I am a writer. What I have to say matters. People are waiting to read my book. I love to write.

How does saying that out loud feel right now? Remember to be positive—and remember that this is lots of *fun!* Okay ... okay ... I'll admit, sometimes writing is difficult. Even noted authors such as Eric Maisel confess that writing can be very demanding work:

For some people, writing is easy. For me, it is very hard. Therefore, I must not be a writer? Rubbish! Sometimes writing is easy, and sometimes writing is hard. So sometimes I will have it easy, and sometimes I will have it hard. Welcome to life.

This should not be discouraging; in fact, it's just the opposite. Even seasoned professionals sometimes find the process more difficult than other times. This is simply part of the job, something that every writer has faced and will continue to face in the future. If you start to feel overwhelmed, remind yourself of this—perhaps even visualize your favorite author having a difficult day, where everything he writes seems like work; then, visualize him sitting down the next day and once again finding the muse. This will happen to you, too. Accept it; it comes with the territory.

STAY SOLUTION-ORIENTED

Along those lines, as you approach the halfway point, tension almost always rears its ugly head. Beginnings are usually fun and endings have a sense of closure and accomplishment, but middles are only halfway done, with half still left to do.

It is very easy to lose steam when you write Act II, to doubt your story's worth, but you must keep writing. *This is a normal reaction.* It is something that should be respected and honored. Work with it, welcome it, and then push right through it. I have had numerous writers tell me that this one secret saved their careers. They thought they weren't meant to be writers when they faced this tension and doubt. Just knowing it was a normal part of the process changed everything for them. Try the following solutions if you need help with fighting off your doubts.

Solution #1: Learn to Write Anywhere

Train yourself to write anytime, anywhere. Set a timer to go off at odd times of the day. Drop whatever you are doing and just write for ten to fifteen minutes. Then stop. After you do this a few times, you will see you actually can write anytime, anywhere. Hey, J.K. Rowling got her idea and outline for Harry Potter while riding a bus. Don't limit yourself or your muse. Be sure to identify the places and times that seemed to work best for you.

WHEN AND WHERE I WROTE WELL

WHEN AND WHERE I WAS EASILY DISTRACTED

Solution #2: Maintain Perspective

Make things interesting for yourself, the writer. You're the one sitting there day after day with this story, after all; make sure you keep something going on in the story that *you* find surprising and enjoyable. Have a supporting character do something crazy that affects the main character. (Think of Kramer on *Seinfeld*: Jerry thinks he is on his way to solving his problem, then—wham!—Kramer's actions throw him a curveball.) The way you feel when writing is usually the way the reader will feel when reading it. So have fun with it.

I remember shooting a student film years ago. We had a short amount of time to get the project done, so we decided to make it a comedy. We had such a blast during the late-night editing sessions! While everyone else in class was lamenting over their serious films, films that would never really be shown anywhere, we were having a grand time in our little editing corner. The point? If you are working on a short story for a small online press, don't try to write a serious, world-changing, add-this-to-the-literary-canon masterpiece. Do your best work, but keep it all in perspective. Save the stress for when it is really called for, like facing a two-week deadline to rewrite a novel for a major house.

Solution #3: Think Big

Come up with an exciting incident to add to the second act, a sort of mini-story within the story. Movies do this all the time. Ever see a montage of events in Act II? Movies often have a mini-story (called a scene sequence) that has a beginning, middle, and end of its own and is resolved rather quickly during Act II. This is not a subplot, but a lighter type of "goings on" that may add drama, may foreshadow the ending, or may show us a bit more about the main character's growth. (More about this in Week 3.) For example: The hero and heroine are trying to get to a boat to find the treasure when, all of a sudden, the hero's mom shows up and forces them to attend his cousin's wedding. He just can't say no to mommy.

BEGINNING	MIDDLE	END

DAY 9

OBJECTIVES

• Plan your post-BIAM celebration now to give you the extra motivation you need for Week 2.

• Check on your main character's motivation and internal conflict.

PLAN YOUR POST-BIAM CELEBRATION!

You are going to write the first half of Act II this week. Some of you should be on your way now, writing every day and feeling pretty darn good about it. Others may start to feel some of the tension we talked about earlier, but now you know what it is you are feeling, and being able to name something gives you power over it, so keep going.

Allow yourself to feel the tension without judgment. Ask yourself, "Can I let go of this feeling?" Breathe. Then ask yourself, "When will I let go of it?" Breathe. Now let go of it. You will be amazed at how breathing deeply can change your state of mind and relax you so the muse can visit.

Regardless of which of the above groups you belong to, read on. Never underestimate the power of positive reinforcement or the power of having something wonderful to look forward to. Human beings naturally move toward pleasure and away from pain. If this BIAM is getting "painful" for you, you just might need some strong "pleasure" to keep you going. This is where your future celebration comes into play. It is a very important exercise, so be sure to complete it. Don't let yourself get dragged down. Feeling fatigued is one of the biggest ways we sabotage ourselves—70 percent of our energy is *emotional* in nature, not *physical*.

Have you ever felt exhausted and then all of a sudden received great news? You immediately perk up and have tons of energy. That energy didn't come from thin air. You always had it; you were just emotionally tired. As soon as you get a positive emotional hit, you access that energy. You need something to look forward to in order to be energized and motivated in life. Looking forward to something gives you energy because it puts you in a positive, expectant state of mind. This is important because the biggest problem BIAMers have is staying motivated!

So what will you do when the 30 days are completed? What do you have to look forward to if you stick with this? What does your heart want most? Do you want to go somewhere? Do you long to see something or someone? Is there something you want to do? Is there something you want to buy? What have you denied yourself lately? Don't worry about what other people will think. Dream big here. Most of all, be truthful, or it won't work as well as it should.

WHAT REWARD I WANT MOST

WHY I HAVEN'T GIVEN THIS TO MYSELF BEFORE

Now you have a reward. You have something to look forward to in two-and-a-half weeks. How does that make you feel? Some of you may feel pressured to get on with it if you have fallen a bit behind, but don't worry about that. Focus on the celebration to come. Feel how wonderful it will be when this draft is written.

Yes, you will have a finished manuscript, but the child inside you (the subconscious part of you where creativity resides) needs something special to motivate her, too. If she is not happy, nobody is happy! This inner child can really put the brakes on if she doesn't get her way, at least a little. Ever see a child flatly refuse to do something? It's not pretty. This is what your inner child, the one who lets you speak to your muse, can be like if you deny her too often. You can't beat yourself up all the time and deny yourself, then sit down and demand to be creative. If you want, you can talk out loud to this inner child and tell her all about the reward, if she will just cooperate with you for the 30 days. (Be sure no one is around to hear you, though!)

A real reward will have many layers to it. Why do you think you want the thing you want? You want to eat a chocolate cake at the end of your BIAM? Why? Because it makes you feel nourished and cared for? It makes you feel good? It reminds you of the cakes your mom used to make on your birthday?

A whole book could be written on this! But for our purpose here, just know that there are usually several reasons why we want what we want. This concept will be clear in a minute when you see how we apply it to your main characters.

Hopefully you took my advice and didn't set your goal way too high. That in itself can be a form of resistance—setting yourself up for failure before you have even begun! Take this celebration reward exercise (or maybe a picture of it if it is a vacation spot, or a brochure or flyer if it is an event you want to attend) and hang it up on the wall. This way, you are reminded of the prize to come in a few weeks.

IDENTIFY CHARACTER MOTIVATION

Now that we've addressed *your* motivation, it's time to get to work on your main character's motivation. Motivation tends to be less of an issue in Act I, since your characters are compelled into action as a direct result of the inciting incident. By Act II, your characters have been kicked around a little, encountered some setbacks, and are likely to be feeling just a tad bit less sure of themselves. This means that you've got to be on the lookout for new and even more compelling reasons for your characters to continue working toward their goals. Remember, everyone—including characters—tends to move toward pleasure and away from pain, so consider the following:

- Are your main characters moving toward pleasure or away from pain? Or both?

- What reward awaits the hero in the end?

- What is motivating the hero to press on?

We are not looking for a generic reply like, "The hero wants to save the village from the bad guys and avenge his friend." Go deeper than that. Ask yourself, "Why does he want this?" You should be to come up with something that ties back to your character's core traits, flaws, and goals. For instance, "The hero needs to feel needed. He needs to save the village to prove his self-worth, and he wants to feel the satisfaction and power of avenging his friend's death."

Now we have a much deeper level at work here. The hero is moving away from the pain of low self-worth and toward the pleasure of being needed and powerful, as well as toward the pleasure of earning admiration from everyone in the village. Doesn't that give you a bit more to write about?

Sometimes it is just the pleasure of doing the right thing ... but why?

- Because the character's mother told him to always do the right thing? (He wants to please his mother and feel like he is worthy of her love.)

- Because the character wants to make up for something he did wrong long ago? (He seeks forgiveness so he can leave the pain of what he did behind him.)

- Because the character wants to believe that good always prevails? (She needs to feel like order has been restored so she can avoid the pain of uncertainty and happenstance.)

Find the deeper meaning. We have all seen the old story where a hero "slays the dragon to win the hand of a princess," but why does he bother? This princess is usually someone who refuses to accept any man but is forced to accept the slayer of the dragon. She is considered unattainable, but will he win other things besides her hand in marriage—self-esteem, admiration, money, power? You decide. These are all rewards the hero can be seeking, but each one carries with it different reasons for attaining it.

Just as good news can lift your spirits and give you more energy, it can also do the same for your characters, so if you have trouble motivating your character into action, give him a jolt of good news. Let's take a look at how big-picture motivation is used in our two examples— *Casablanca* and *Dracula*. (Remember, too, that smaller motivations are a part of every scene.)

CASABLANCA

Rick wants to do the right thing, but why? He knows he can't take care of Ilsa the way Laszlo can; he knows Laszlo won't be able to fight the good fight against the Nazis if Ilsa walks out on him now; and he knows deep inside that what they shared is over. He has spent so much time in turmoil over the way she abandoned him, he just couldn't go through that again ... and he's unsure whether he could put another man through it. In the beginning, Rick doesn't seem to care about anyone or anything, but the truth is, he is just a broken man who is afraid to care about anyone. Seeing Ilsa again and getting the answers he needs exhilarates him, but her profession of love still leaves an important question unanswered: Is the "right" thing to do to follow his heart? Or are there bigger concerns than his own—their own—happiness?

DRACULA

The Count wants to "win" the girl—though his definition of winning may be different from ours— but *why*? He believes she is his long-lost love. He believes she belongs to him, and he wants to save her from death and human frailty. He doesn't want to be alone anymore. A part of him also wants to show the other men who are trying to destroy him that he is all-powerful and gets what he wants.

When thinking about your own characters, remember that motivations tend to evolve as circumstances change, small goals are accomplished, and new problems arise. A character's motivation needs to be clear to readers at all times, and this motivation must be scene-specific and tailor-made for the individual character. When exploring motivation options for a specific character, consider his flaws, as well as his goals. Think about the various small goals he may have already accomplished, and the different types of resistance he faces in the specific scene you're writing, as well as those he's likely to encounter throughout the course of the story. Once you've identified these variables, brainstorm different motivating factors until you find one that excites you and fits with the rest of your story.

CHARACTER MOTIVATORS

Scene	Character	Flaws and Goals	Resistance	Direct Motivation

DAY 10

The ultimate measure of a person is not where they stand in moments of comfort and convenience, but where they stand in times of challenge and controversy.

—Dr. Martin Luther King, Jr.

OBJECTIVES

• Fill out the Plot Snapshot worksheet.

• Explore the use of cliffhangers to beef up a sagging middle.

DEVELOP A PLOT SNAPSHOT

The start of Act II is a great place to pause and evaluate just how well your plot is evolving, and that's where the Plot Snapshot worksheet comes into play. You don't want to go too far into Act II before filling this out. Even those of you who hate outlines and structure should like this one. It's a quick and easy snapshot of a very basic story element—the three big events. You don't want to focus on this in Act I, as you have enough to do in Week 1! You will probably come up with more ideas, as you write Act II fast anyway. (Somehow, writing fast usually makes you more creative ... maybe because there's less time for obsessive second-guessing.)

So now that you have written some of the story and can really see it taking off, fill out the Plot Snapshot worksheet. It may also provide some excitement for you, as it can spark many wonderful new ideas. The different ways of looking at story elements seem to help different types of writers. Sometimes we get too bogged down by the explanations and terminology teachers have been using for so long that we just need a new way of looking at a story to inspire us a bit.

Every story should have at least three big events to keep things interesting for the reader. These events can be as dramatic or lighthearted as you want them to be, no judgment about content here! Also, these three big events aren't "turning points" as we've been defining them, or at least they don't have to be. For example, the scene in *Casablanca* where Ilsa comes to Rick's apartment isn't merely a turning point in the plot; it *deepens* the plot, deepens our understanding of who the characters are, and remains one of the most emotional and unforgettable scenes in the film. Just make sure you have at least three interesting events during your story. Some writers choose to have one event per act, but many writers put two events in Act II to keep it moving, with the third event as the finale. Have *six* events if you wish; three is the usual minimum.

Note also that these events are different from genre events that will be discussed later (e.g., if you are writing a romance novel, this is not about having three love scenes—that relates to expectations of genre). These events are about moving the plot forward and making things interesting. So romance novelists might have three big events that complicate things for the lovers in general (which will naturally have an effect when you *do* get to those genre scenes).

If you can't find three big events in your story, then something is off. Even in character-driven stories, you need some type of event to have the opportunity to reveal "character." You don't have to have an explosion or a car chase; the event can be as big or subtle as you want. Maybe a tomboy heroine is forced to buy a silk gown and get a makeover. (That should reveal some character, all right.) It just has to be a scene of interest to your readers ... and of interest to the bigger story and character arcs.

PLOT SNAPSHOT

Describe, in detail, the first event that happens in this story.

Describe what this event accomplishes. (Does it advance plot, reveal character, make readers feel specific emotions, etc.?)

Setting	Characters Involved	Conflicts That Arise and Their Effect

Describe how the conflicts that arise affect the characters and plot in both the short- and long-term of your story.

Describe, in detail, the second event that happens in this story.

Describe what this event accomplishes.

Setting	Characters Involved	Conflicts That Arise and Their Effect

Describe how the conflicts that arise affect the characters and plot in both the short- and long-term of your story.

Describe, in detail, the third event that happens in this story.

Describe what this event accomplishes.

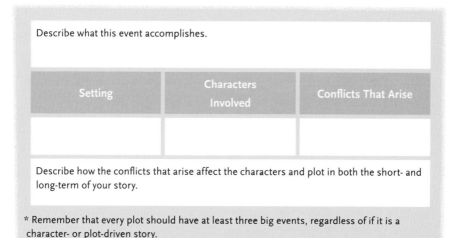

Setting	Characters Involved	Conflicts That Arise

Describe how the conflicts that arise affect the characters and plot in both the short- and long-term of your story.

* Remember that every plot should have at least three big events, regardless of if it is a character- or plot-driven story.

INSERT CLIFFHANGERS

Cliffhangers can really beef up a sagging second act, and they're great for when you find yourself without any obvious next steps. You are nearing the halfway mark and don't know what to do with the story next. The last week is easy—it's the ending, the big climax and resolution—but this middle section needs some help to keep it going. How will you get through Week 2 and keep readers interested in the remaining part of Act II next week? It can seem so daunting.

The answer is to come up with an event, perhaps one of the three you just created, and delay paying it off. Set up the event so that readers truly don't know if things will work out. There has to be a question in readers' minds about what will happen next. Some classic cliffhangers include:

- the ticking clock (the hero must do something in a certain amount of time, and readers don't know if it is possible to accomplish);

- the character on the verge of making a hasty major decision (perhaps she doesn't have all the information yet and readers want her to wait, but it doesn't look like she will);

- the interruption, either in the form of another character or an event, that throws the heroine offtrack (the heroine is about to find her husband upstairs cheating with another woman when her neighbor stops by to talk, keeping her downstairs, and readers don't know if she will go upstairs and finally learn the truth ... ringing phones and tea kettles usually fall into this category, and for this reason should be avoided); and

- the unexpected problem that pops up just when the resolution seems on the horizon (the hero and heroine seem likely to get together, which would mean "the end," when numerous problems are dropped into their laps, and readers now question if it will work out).

The goal here is to leave readers wondering about what could possibly happen next, so that they won't be able to put the book down. You have to be careful that you make this seem seamless, though. It has to feel natural and organic to the plot; otherwise, readers will get upset with you and feel manipulated. Hey, if it were easy, every book would be a page-turner! You are creating anticipation in readers. This anticipation has to be paid off at some point.

So when and how do you cut back to the cliffhanger? That's another choice you have to make on your own. You don't want to wait too long, or it will seem as if the entire plot has come to a screeching halt. If you go back too quickly, you will lose your opportunity to keep readers hooked. This is why writing is an art form. You have to feel the story, feel the pacing, understand the genre, and make these decisions.

Watch a dramatic TV show to see how they use cliffhangers before commercial breaks, or watch some movie trailers to see how they try to entice you into the theater.

CLIFFHANGER BRAINSTORM

Identify and describe a scene in the first part of Act II that has cliffhanger potential.

Quickly outline three cliffhanger ideas and their resolutions.

For each idea, describe what you will cut to immediately after the cliffhanger.

For each idea, describe how you will return to the cliffhanger to resolve it.

Describe how each cliffhanger option will affect your characters and your plot both in the short- and long-term of your story.

DAY 11

All you have to do is look straight and see the road, and when you see it, don't sit looking at it—walk.

—AYN RAND

OBJECTIVES

• Spice up your story with ideas you get from today's brainstorming questions.

• Make every word count.

• Keep writing Act II.

• Remember to refer to the plot outline sheets, and make sure you have your Week 2 traditional elements in place.

Your goal is almost half completed! Push yourself a bit more this week. Steal an extra fifteen minutes from somewhere for writing. You can do it! This is important. Once you are on a roll, it is hard to stop. A good first two weeks will keep you going for the final two weeks. You're reaching a very important milestone.

SPICE UP YOUR STORY

Answer the questions in the following plot, character, and setting brainstorm worksheets to generate ideas, create more details, or spice up your story. You just never know when you may find a use for some of these ideas. They often just come pouring through as you write fast. You are making decisions in these worksheets that your subconscious will use later on, when you are absorbed in the act of writing fast. So don't think you are wasting any time here if you don't come up with amazing ideas; everything gets logged into the subconscious, and new associations and ideas are then developed. Everything in BIAM has a purpose!

PLOT BRAINSTORM

What specifically in Act II will make your readers care about the hero's goal?

What interests you most about Act II? (Something better!)

What is the wildest thing that can happen as Act II progresses?

If you had to shock your readers in Act II, what could you do?

What are three different turning points you might throw into Act II to keep it interesting (if needed)?

CHARACTER BRAINSTORM

How will your main character grow (or perhaps resist change) in Act II?

What fears will your main character have to overcome in Act II?

Which supporting characters will play a major role in Act II, and how?

Will any new characters be introduced in Act II? If so, why? How will you foreshadow them?

What does your main character do differently in Act II?

Does your main character show another side of himself in Act II—a side that has always been there, but readers may not have really noticed before? If so, do you properly foreshadow this in Act I?

Soon your main character will be facing the final confrontation; is he up to it yet, or does he have more to learn in Act II?

Will your main character have to lie or cheat in Act II?

What have you learned about your character's ethics by Act II? Would he swear? Would he hurt one to save many? How far would he go to get the job done?

If your character's house were burning down, what object do you think he would save? Why?

What event in Act II makes your character question whether his goal is really worth it, and why? What motivates him onward in spite of this doubt?

How could the antagonist have a bigger presence in Act II?

Does the antagonist have any phobias, weaknesses, or shortcomings that come out in Act II?

SETTING BRAINSTORM

What props could you put into Act II to spice it up?

Does the setting affect the plot progression in Act II at all? Does it cause any additional obstacles?

Is there a new setting you can introduce in Act II?

Can you change a setting in Act II and throw the characters off? (For instance, the bank they planned to rob has been turned into a restaurant, and all their plans to break into the safe are foiled.)

Have new characters taken over a setting in Act II? (For example, the government has occupied a town, and now the hero can't pass the checkpoints to reach his destination.)

BALANCE DESCRIPTION BY MAKING EVERY WORD COUNT

Descriptive writing explains a person, place, or thing in great detail. Now, you don't want to describe *everything* in your novel in great detail; modern readers couldn't handle it. Yes, I know some classics may do this, but you can't write fast and stop to describe every detail as you go. You need to pick the moments in your story where you really want to paint a picture for readers, or where you really want readers to feel something and then go for it. Let me ask you this: Which of the following is more interesting?

Cathy bit into an apple.

Or:

> Cathy sunk her pearly whites into a slice of fried green jalapenos.

Which paints a better picture?

> It was a hot day, and Sam didn't feel like walking down that old dirt road yet again.

Or:

> The heat rose from the ground, creating a rippling effect through the air. Sam stared down that long dirt road without moving a muscle. Not a sound was heard. The animals knew to find shelter on days like this. Sam just had no sense at all.

I assume you picked the second version of each. These are examples of why it is important to make every word count. Be specific. Picture the scene you are working on in your mind (hopefully you have your worksheets filled out with all kinds of details and ideas to work with here). What about this scene relates to the plot or character? Does it matter that it is a hot day? Maybe, maybe not. Will describing the heat reveal something about the character? It could. Does it at least make the scene more interesting? It better!

Don't just arbitrarily have your character grab an apple; why bother? But if she is a chocolate junkie and her doctor is making her eat healthy, then it makes sense. Otherwise, be more descriptive and come up with something unusual here and there. Memorable characters are those with some quirks. Remember the Character Story and Character Snapshot worksheets you filled out on Day 4? Now is the time to check in on them again and make sure you haven't forgotten any of your great ideas. If you didn't have any great ideas then, create some now, now that you know the character a bit more.

Think about the five (or six) senses—sight, smell, taste, sound, and touch, and either extrasensory perception or imagination—and how they can be used in the scene. Which ones would this character use in this scene? Which ones are most important given the scene's unique circumstances? Here are some ideas of how to incorporate sense:

- Is your character alone in the mountains? Being able to hear an approaching animal or the voices of a rescue party might save her life.

- Is it important in the final scene that readers know your hero hates Velcro? Then let him feel a piece in this scene.

- Do readers need to know that the hero makes poor decisions? Then send him out in 110-degree weather when all the other animals are smart enough to find shelter.

- Is the heroine psychic? Then maybe her sixth sense comes into play and she feels another character's emotions and thoughts as she enters the scene.

Let's take it a step further. What inanimate elements are in the scene that you could make animate? For example:

The mist rose, caressing Jen's cheek as it wound its gray fingers through her curly blonde hair.

The mist takes on an active, animate role here and really comes alive for readers. We can feel how heavy the mist must be to wind through her hair as if it were the fingers of a person.

The sea was jealous that day ...

The tree loomed over him, laughing at his predicament ...

Find those moments in your story, usually in Act II because that is the "body" of the story, and give readers some vivid details to make the story rich.

DAY 12

A [person] is like a tea bag. You never know strong she is until she gets into hot water.

—ELEANOR ROOSEVELT

OBJECTIVES

- Intensify the main problem a bit with a barrier, complication, or new situation.

- Build the temporary triumph for your main character that wraps up Act II, Part 1.

INTENSIFY YOUR CHARACTER'S MAIN PROBLEM

You've been developing your character's main story problem since completing the At-A-Glance Outline back on Day 3—and you'd probably been thinking about it even before then. (And good for you if you have!) Of course, as you know by now, starting your story with a compelling problem is only the first step. You've got to keep upping the ante, intensifying the conflict as the problem continues to grow and grow. You do this by weaving in believable and nuanced barriers, complications, and situations. I outlined each of these at the start of Week 2, so let's only do a quick refresher here and then get to writing:

- Barriers occur when the character tries something that doesn't work. The action is stopped for a moment and readers wonder, "What will the character do?"

- Complications are action points that don't pay off immediately. The hero is busy with the main plot line and all of a sudden a new element, character, or conflict, drops into the mix.

- Situations use one of the dramatic predicaments to move the story forward and add tension.

Pull out your earlier outline and plot worksheets and review your story problem's charted course. You're going to deepen the well now by adding in a mixture of the three different types of conflict just described. Push yourself and see what happens.

CONFLICT BRAINSTORM

	Scene	Characters Involved	Result
Barrier			
Complication			
Situation			
Barrier			
Complication			
Situation			

Don't feel too bad about making life harder for your characters. Sometimes we just love our characters too darn much! Other times we identify with them too deeply. This is what makes conflict such a chore. You don't want your heroine to face having her son hit by a car; you just can't bring yourself to write it, but you know in your gut that it has to be done. You know the story calls for it. Remember: You are doing your entire story, and your character, an injustice if you *don't* write it.

Would kids still love Harry Potter so much if his aunt and uncle were nice and loving toward him? No. When his aunt and uncle make him sleep under the stairs and treat him worse than the family pet, readers empathize with him, readers want him to succeed. The main thing is to make sure you have enough conflict in your story to keep the characters motivated, keep them moving toward the end goal. Conflict allows readers to identify with your beloved character. You are writing for an audience, aren't you? Use conflict to show them how wonderful this character is. Let your character show the world how he can shine. Give him conflict so he can rise above it. Evaluate your story's conflict by asking yourself the following questions:

Are you having any trouble with conflict? If so, why?

What conflicts have you set up for your characters?

How can you make those conflicts even worse for your characters?

DEVELOP YOUR TEMPORARY TRIUMPH

The temporary triumph comes at the end of Act II, Part 1 (the halfway mark). This is when the main character thinks she has achieved her goal, but unbeknownst to her, there is a reversal just waiting around the corner. (As we wait for the reversal, the subplot could come into the picture for a while.) The temporary triumph makes the character feel as if he has attained his goal and the story is over. He achieves something great and thinks, "Whew! That was tough, but I succeeded." Then he turns the corner and *wham!* He's right back to square one, or worse. Here are some examples:

- He found the lost treasure! (*temporary triumph*) But wait—it's only fool's gold. (*reversal*)

- She got the job of her dreams and can now support her family! (*temporary triumph*) Oh no, it was just a scam and she already quit her old crappy job. (*reversal*)

- He found the love of his life and can let himself love again after going through a horrible divorce! (*temporary triumph*) Wait— she's already married and not interested in anything long-term. (*reversal*)

- She discovered a cure for baldness! (*temporary triumph*) Oops—it has horrible side effects and her company is being sued. (*reversal*)

TEMPORARY TRIUMPH BRAINSTORM

Scene	Characters Involved	Temporary Triumph	Reversal	Ramifications (Long- and Short-Term)

If you are having trouble figuring out what your story's temporary triumph should be, remember that it needs to push the main character toward his ultimate goal. Look at where you want that character to be in the end of the story. How can you use the temporary triumph to support that ending?

Now come up with two ways to show the temporary triumph:

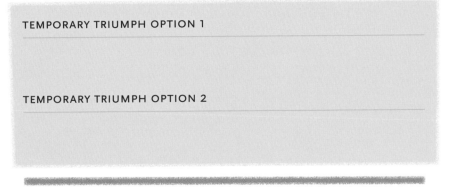

TEMPORARY TRIUMPH OPTION 1

TEMPORARY TRIUMPH OPTION 2

DAY 13

OBJECTIVES

• Deepen your crucial subplots.

• Take the Domino Scene Test.

CRAFT YOUR SUBPLOTS

Even if you thought you identified exactly what all your subplots would be right after you completed the At-A-Glance Outline, you may find that a few new ones are popping up as you move through your book. Why does this tend to happen? Easy—subplots should help support the main plot. Although one of the rules of a BIAM is to leave out subplots in favor of cementing the plot (since subplots are usually the first things to change in a rewrite), as you near the halfway mark, you probably have some good idea regarding what to do in your subplots. You can continue take notes for later use, or, if you're ahead of the game and want to work on the subplots a bit, go for it! Sometimes they inform and affect the direction of the main plot, and, thus, sometimes you need to craft them bit to keep your momentum going.

Remember, subplots support the main plot in one or more ways, typically by:

- supporting and advancing the main storyline;

- revealing character;

- illustrating the theme (the best subplots are those that reinforce the theme ... theme will be more fully discussed on Day 15);

- mirroring the main storyline in a smaller way;

- creating conflict and complications for the main storyline;

- evoking emotions in readers; and

- relieving tension for readers (especially in the horror genre— readers need a break now and then).

Subplots really do have a lot of work to do. That is why they're usually best left to a bare minimum when writing a book in 30 days. Besides, if they're probably going to change along the way, as most subplots tend to do, you don't want to spend too much precious time on them.

Still, though, you do want to have some idea of what your subplots are going to be and how they're going to inform and complement your story. This will be particularly helpful to you as your characters and main storyline begin to fully take shape. That's why keeping track of your subplot ideas throughout your story is vitally important, and why sketching out your options at this stage might be a good idea. What subplot ideas do you have, and what function do they serve? Remember also that all subplots need to be resolved by the end of the story. How will you resolve them?

SUBPLOT BRAINSTORM

Subplot	Function	Characters Involved	Subplot Resolution

EVALUATE YOUR SCENE SEQUENCE

Know what happens when you line up a series of dominoes and then tap the first one? They all fall down, one after the other. However, take one of the middle dominoes away and the rest won't fall—right? It's the same with your story. You line up all your scenes, and the characters proceed through them, one after the other. Take one of those scenes out, and the rest of the scenes fall apart behind it. Or, at least, they should.

The point here is to make sure you have your scenes in the correct order and that each scene is fed by the one (or, more likely, *ones*) preceding it. Your book should be ordered as meticulously as that stretch of dominoes, all perfectly positioned to reveal, once they fall, an intricate, beautiful pattern. But if even one of them is out of place, you run the risk of breaking the momentum, and that beautiful big picture you have in mind might never come to be.

Each scene should have a purpose in the story, a reason for being: to advance plot, reveal character, divulge information, something. If not, it doesn't need to be there, at least in its current form; either get rid of it or give it a purpose. As you write, be aware of how one scene ends and the next one begins. This is usually easy when you write fast; you don't have a lot of time to lose track of what you are doing.

An easy way to see if your scene has a purpose is to ask yourself, "What would happen if I removed this scene?" If a scene or two after it would fall apart, or not make sense, then you need that scene. If you take it out and it has zero effect on your story ... well, then, it likely shouldn't have been there in the first place.

Test your scenes by completing the Domino Scene Test. Write a one- or two-line scene summary for each of the scenes you've written so far. As you do this, it should be clear to you how each scene supports the next. If one scene doesn't seem to be pulling its weight, be prepared to revise or cut it later.

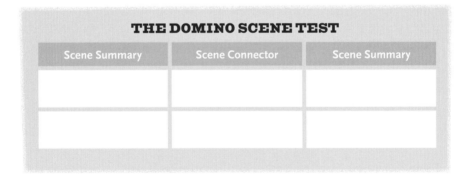

THE DOMINO SCENE TEST

Scene Summary	Scene Connector	Scene Summary

DAY 14

There's no scarcity of opportunity to make a living at what you love.
There is only a scarcity of resolve to make it happen.

—WAYNE DYER

OBJECTIVE

• Uncover those story holes for this portion of Act II.

FIND AND FILL STORY HOLES

Mark any holes you find on the research and notes sheets for the re-write. This quick holes check is just to make sure you are not going too far off track. We will visit these again in Week 4.

Holes are any areas in the story that are not believable, something that just doesn't quite make sense, something that is missing, or something that doesn't seem to fit.

Ever watch a film and think:

• "Why the heck would that character care about that?" The story is missing some explanation, backstory, or emotional depth.

• "Why would he say (or do) that?" The story is missing some important characterization here.

• "I can't possibly accept that characters can do that, no way." The story is missing some story rules; the "world" the characters inhabit is not well defined.

You can't just throw in a superhero without some sort of explanation. Everything in your story needs to be clear, the world needs to be built, the characters need to act in character, and the plot needs to make sense. Sometimes it is just a case of the writer knowing a lot about a story and not realizing all that information is not on the page so readers will understand it. You don't want to give too much backstory, but you *do* want to make sure everything is believable. Ultimately, you will want someone you trust to read your story and look for holes, but that is easier said than done, so use the following checklists to evaluate your work.

CHARACTER HOLE CHECKLIST

☐ Does a character act "out of character"? If so, why? How can you convey the reasons he is acting out of character so you don't lose your readers?

☐ Should you put him back "into character"? What would that mean? Require?

☐ Have characters gone missing—dropped out of your storyline?

☐ Do you have too many characters on stage at once?

☐ Are characters reacting more than acting?

PLOT HOLE CHECKLIST

☐ Does the plot slow down?

☐ Are portions of the plot too confusing?

☐ Are you trying to do too much in any one scene?

☐ Did you set up numerous subplots and characters in the beginning only to find you can't keep up with all of them now?

☐ Did you set up something that doesn't seem to be paying off?

BELIEVABILITY HOLE CHECKLIST

☐ Does the villain do something that is just too over-the-top?

☐ Is your hero's commitment to his goal still believable?

☐ Are all character actions and reactions motivated?

RESEARCH HOLE CHECKLIST

☐ Do you know enough about the town and setting you are using? Are there any additional details you can add to make the location more realistic?

☐ Are there specific things you need to learn more about, like a weapon or tool?

☐ Are your details in line with your story's time period? For instance, are the clothes, vehicles, etc., all true to the era in which your story takes places?

WEEK 2 WRAP-UP

Congratulations! This is the end of the second week.

- Did you say the mantra every day?

- Did you stick to the five secrets and not rewrite while working?

- Have you done all the exercises?

- Did you face any tension?

- Have you kept a list of things you need to research later on?

- Are family and friends helping or hurting your process? You may need to talk with them about it. If they are helping, then let them know how much you appreciate it!

PROGRESS TRACKER

Week 1: 25%	Week 2: 50%	Week 3: 75%	Week 4: 100%

Congratulations! You've hit the halfway mark. Take a moment right now to look back and see how far you've come. Have you ever written so many pages before in two weeks? *Now* do you believe you can do it? You have proven to yourself that you can do this, so don't lose steam now. You have no more excuses. You can do it. You just *did* it!

Maybe you are thinking, "But I messed up Day 3 and didn't meet my overall word count for the week and ... and ... and ..." Stop! Not everyone is perfect the first time (or even second time) around. We all start from different places with different distractions, responsibilities, and blocks, so this process will be a bit different for everyone. Some of you will start off well but finish a little lackluster and vice versa. It doesn't matter. Just finish! Stick with it. Keep your fingers on the keyboard and write.

Who knows? You may be a whiz when it comes to the rewrite stage. Or you may whiz through the first draft and go through hell with the rewrite stage. Forget about it. Writing every day is the important thing. Don't judge yourself or overanalyze your process; you shouldn't have time for it. Above all, remember to stay positive and to have fun with it. You're your first reader, so make the book that *you* want to keep reading.

This week will focus on the second half of Act II—the reversal, the dark moment, and the second turning point. Again, these aren't meant to be rigid constraints, but guidelines that will help you maintain both forward motion and focus. There are also some great worksheets for this week to help you stay on track.

TRADITIONAL STORY STRUCTURE: ACT II, PART 2

In Act I, we presented our hero with an initial problem and then complicated things by introducing a secondary, more serious problem, thus forming the major conflict of our story and creating our first big turning point. In the first part of Act II, we intensified the conflict, first by adding new barriers, complications, and situations for our hero to contend with, and then by raising the hero's hopes with an all-too-temporary triumph. So where does that leave *us*, the writers, in the second part of Act II? Remember in the last chapter when we talked about how readers might worry things will get worse for the hero before they get better? Well, the readers were right.

• **Reversal:** Now the problem worsens. The triumph is no longer a true triumph, and the main character's trials are not over by a long shot. The reversal can happen several different ways. Some of them include:

  • new information coming into play;

  • a dramatic situation occurring;

  • another character turning on the main character;

  • helpers and friends giving up on the main character, abandoning him;

  • a meeting place changing at the last minute, or a task going awry;

  • the main character's thinking shown to be mistaken, misguided, or just plain wrong; and

  • the villain becoming the good guy, or the good guy becoming a bad guy—a misreading of one character by other characters.

• **Dark Moment:** The reversal leads to the dark moment. The main character fails (or at least seems to), or the main character thinks things are just too much to handle. Think of action films where the hero has a confrontation with the villain and barely gets out alive. The problem gets worse for the main character, and his goal is pushed further out of reach. We wonder if he will ever succeed because it seems as if all is lost.

Soon after Ilsa professes her love for Rick, Laszlo stumbles into Rick's bar, wounded from having just escaped certain arrest. Laszlo asks Rick for the letters of transit so that he and Ilsa can escape, and he tries to use Rick's love for Ilsa to convince him to hand over the letters. But just then, German officers storm Rick's and take Laszlo into custody. The next day, Rick visits Louis and tells him that, if he lets Laszlo go, Rick can arrange for Laszlo to be caught with the stolen letters, a charge that would put him away indefinitely, so that Rick can leave the country with Ilsa. The reversal, as far as the audience can see, appears to be Rick's, who seems to be selling out Laszlo so that he can be with Ilsa; love might win, but at a high moral price. The audience is made uncomfortable by the fact that, after everything that's happened, Rick still appears to be looking out only for himself.

DRACULA

Harker, Van Helsing, and Lucy's former suitors set off to find the Count's store of Transylvanian soil to destroy it, but, unbeknownst to them, Renfield, a mental patient in contact with the Count, leads the Count to the hospital where Mina had been sequestered. The men arrive back at the hospital moments too late; the Count has bitten Mina, seduced her, and her fate seems sealed. She is—or soon will be—a vampire herself ... a dark moment, indeed. Mina's only hope now is for the men to track down the Count and kill him, freeing her from his grip, but the clock is ticking.

• **Turning Point:** This turning point accomplishes the same things as the first turning point at the end of Act I. The one difference is that the main character is usually forced into making a decision that propels this turning point.

CASABLANCA

Rick sells his café to his rival, something he swore he'd never do, and is putting his business in order. It appears that Rick is preparing to set up Laszlo exactly as he told Louis he would. But will he really go through with the plan, even if the goal is to be with Ilsa? Will he sell out Laszlo to find his own happiness?

DRACULA

The sacred dirt from his homeland effectively sterilized by the men chasing him, the Count's weaknesses catch up with him, and he must get home to lay in fresh dirt. If the men can catch the Count before he reaches his home soil and his castle, there may be hope for Mina. But if not ...

DAY 15

When you have many excuses not to do your work, ask yourself what guarantee you have of another chance to do what needs to be done. Time lost is lost for good ... Wake up and stop the excuses; they never made sense before and do not make sense now. Laziness and procrastination have never worked in a sound and helpful way. It is only sound and helpful to get things moving.

—The Venerable Khenpo Karthar Rinpoche

OBJECTIVE

• Now that you know more about your story and characters, it's time to develop your theme using the Theme Spider.

HONE YOUR THEME

Very few writers know their theme before they start writing. Instead, it is usually a subconscious thing that goes on behind the scenes as you write. When you hit the halfway mark, you usually uncover what your theme is on a conscious level. You start to see a pattern of symbols, ideas, or messages in your story.

But if you don't know your theme, then you may be in a little trouble. The number one—okay, maybe the number *two*—reason writers get stuck halfway through their story is that they don't have a theme at work anywhere. Theme is what we all write for. Theme is your unique perspective and expression; it is part of your voice.

If I asked ten writers to write a short story about a girl who goes to the corner store, each story would be executed differently, depending on the unique theme each writer wants to convey. One writer might choose to make it a rainy day with tons of gang members and drug addicts in the girl's path. Another writer may choose to make it a hazy day with no one on the streets for miles; the girl is totally alone. A third writer might make it a sunny day and have the girl pick up her friends along the way; maybe the girl ends up spending the money on candy and knows she will get into trouble for it.

Don't each of these versions convey a different theme or message? Yet they are all from the same storyline—a girl goes to the corner store. The writers don't start out saying, "I will write about fate and how dangerous the world is," or "I will write about how we are all alone in this world," or "I want to convey the joys of childhood friendships." No, they just started writing, not really consciously understanding exactly why they made the choices they made in the beginning.

Halfway through, your theme should start to become clear; now you can try to foster that theme in your story and make sure it is clear in the end. This way, readers will feel satisfied when they are done with your book.

A theme is what readers get out of reading your story—a message, a lesson, a new way of looking at things. Themes can come in many different forms, but the key is to figure out what readers gain from reading the story *and* why you wrote it. Why did you make all your main characters aliens, for example? Did you want to talk about issues of not fitting in? Or issues about how we treat those who are different from us?

What is the issue or message for you here? A part of you wanted to make those characters aliens (not fitting in), or set the story in a small town (community), or show the gritty side of a hero (imperfection), or kill off the downtrodden friend in a senseless act of violence (fate) … so *why*?

Although it may seem like arbitrary decisions to non-writers, writers know that no creative choice is mere happenstance. Our subconscious mind speaks to us via symbols, feelings, and metaphors. This is why we make these creative choices and why we are usually not sure why something in our writing *has* to be a certain way: "I feel like this character needs to do X," or "I've always pictured the heroine with short black hair, wild eyes, and a long scar on her cheek."

Writers are not so self-absorbed! We feel things need to be a certain way because the theme is telling us it should be a certain way. If your reviewer or editor doesn't understand where you are coming from and wants you to change things, then you can bet you are not conveying your theme enough.

Remember, theme does not covey what will happen in the plot. Theme does not care about the ending or the character's goals. Theme is subtle, more like a feeling or a reason behind the choices made by a writer. You have your plot, but the choices you make when telling that plot usually convey a theme.

Here's another thing to think about: What's the title of your story? Surprisingly, you can usually find your theme within your working title. The subconscious does speak to us, though it sometimes takes us a while to hear it.

Feel free to wait until the rewrite stage to spend a lot of time on theme if you want to. Though again, if you've given the characters and situations the depth they deserve, the theme is likely already there, waiting for you to build it up.

The Theme Spider Worksheet

What's the theme of *your* story? To start developing an answer to this essential question, take a look at the worksheet on page 165. Write your main ideas for your work-in-progress in the boxes. Write your actual theme in the center square. You probably won't be able to address every element of the Theme Spider at this stage, and that's perfectly fine. Just check back from time to time and update the worksheet as your story progresses. This will help you to make sure that your theme is thoroughly embedded into your story. Before you start the worksheet, though, let's take a closer look at the points you'll need to consider:

- Why you wrote this story and what you like about your story both tell you something about the theme. While we may like the plot events and think they are entertaining, we like our stories and are compelled to write them because of theme.

- The personal message area is for you to articulate as best you can the personal message this story holds for you when you think about it. This is usually what you think the theme is, but you may be wrong. So hold this answer up to the rest of the sheet and see if it fits. There may be a disconnect here between what you think the theme is and what it actually is.

- What you want readers to get from reading this story is all about what your goal is as the writer of this story. Just as the character has a goal in the end, so do you, the writer, have a goal to reach in the end. Let's make sure you know what it is—it is usually also part of the theme.

- The choices you make to ensure that your theme is woven into the fabric of your story are going to be very, very important to the overall quality of your work. Think about the conscious efforts you've made so far to express your theme and how else you might do this moving forward.

- You're about halfway through your book right now. Think about all the scenes you've already written that somehow convey your theme. Are they working? How do they affect the theme, and how might you play with this in future scenes?

- You need to have a good understanding of how your main character and your theme are intertwined. In *Casablanca*, we have theme of "escaping the past," with Rick trying to forget about the love he felt for Ilsa, and Laszlo and Ilsa literally trying to escape to a new life.

- Think about the props you use to express your theme. In *Casablanca*, the airplanes and the songs sung in the café all work to convey the theme. In *Dracula*, the names of places and the ships, blood motifs, and Catholic iconography are all used as symbols in this story to convey the themes of purity and purity lost.

- Your theme should be subtle, but not so subtle that readers don't even notice it. Be careful, though, not to get too preachy—that's likely to push readers away. Remember that *message* is not the same as *moral* (or even the same as having a moral).

- The "Notes" section is anything else you want to include—notes on scenes you'll need to revise later, ideas for future scenes, etc.

THEME SPIDER

Why you wrote this story:	What you like about this story:	What you want readers to get:
Props used to express your theme:	**Theme:**	How your main character and theme are connected:
Places where your theme is too overt or too subtle:		Scenes crucial to conveying your theme:
Personal message you want your story to convey:	Choices made to ensure your theme gets conveyed:	Notes:

Looking over your Theme Spider Worksheet, do you see any patterns? Hopefully you do. You don't want to have too many different themes working at once. Are there a lot of thoughts and images that convey something about life, humanity, culture, relationships, or morals? (There should be—theme is usually found in such things.) It is much easier to write about (and read about) one or two themes than five to ten themes! Write about *something*, not everything.

Now revisit the Theme Spider again and see if you need to make any changes to your story. Do you have enough examples, symbols, characters, and props to support the message you want to get across? Is there something else you can add to your story to get this theme across to your readers more clearly?

Theme building is an art. It is best to let the subconscious work it out for a bit before you consciously try to figure it out. This is why we waited until Week 3 to examine it. What has your subconscious already told you about the theme you want to write? If you can't find a theme at all, are you working on a project you like? It is very rare not to have any hint of a theme at all ... keep looking.

DAY 16

The artist is not identical with the process of creation; he is aware that he is subordinate to his work or stands outside it, as though he were a second person; or as though a person other than himself had fallen within the magic circle of an alien will.

—CARL JUNG

OBJECTIVE

- Develop a sequence to spice things up or to develop the characters.

SEQUENCE YOUR SCENES

Getting through the second act can be hard. One trick from screenwriting is to use a *sequence* to keep things moving. A sequence is a group of scenes that makes up its own mini-story inside the story.

Let's say your hero and heroine have run away together. They are hiding from the bad guys, but you know they will go back home to finish the storyline and nothing too catastrophic will happen here. You could have the hero and heroine explore something unrelated to the main plotline for a couple of scenes, usually something that will reveal character. This "something" can be a sequence of scenes that has a beginning, middle, and end of its own. Here's a sequence example:

Beginning: The hero searches for some ammunition. He and the heroine go into a warehouse. Someone is walking around outside, so they have to hide out for a while.

Middle: They look for ammo, get to know each other a bit, and the hero saves the heroine from falling off a ladder. They kiss, and intimacy develops between them. Their relationship moves to the next level.

End: They react to this new level of intimacy (perhaps by pulling away from each other). They grab the ammo and escape.

Sequences are used a lot to open films as in *Gladiator* and *Saving Private Ryan*. Very often, scene sequences are fast-paced, so you need to find those elements in the beginning, middle, and end that you should focus on to get your point across. This is especially true if you are revealing important information. Remember, though, not to lose sight of your main storyline during the scene sequence. It should still be in the back of the hero's mind, informing his decisions.

(Note, though, that sequences are different from fantasies. Fantasies or dreams don't have much to do with the main plot and are usually used to depict a character's inner life in a way that outward action can't. They often don't have a beginning, middle, and end ... do *your* fantasies?)

Now it's your turn to develop or improve your own scene sequences using the following worksheet.

SCENE SEQUENCER

SEQUENCE SYNOPSIS

Beginning	Setting	Characters	Crucial Elements

Middle	Setting	Characters	Crucial Elements

End	Setting	Characters	Crucial Elements

DAY 17

Another luxury for an idle imagination is the writer's own feeling about the work. There is neither a proportional relationship, nor an inverse one, between a writer's estimation of a work in progress and its actual quality. The feeling that the work is magnificent, and the feeling that it is abominable, are both mosquitoes to be repelled, ignored, or killed, but not indulged.

—ANNIE DILLARD

OBJECTIVES

• Craft your reversal so you can set up your second turning point.

• Keep an eye on pacing so you are not overwhelmed during the rewrite.

CRAFT YOUR REVERSAL

As we discussed in the chapter opening, the reversal comes toward the end of Act II (it sets up the second turning point). This reversal turns the story around a bit. The hero thought he was successful, but now he sees he was wrong.

Go over your reversal and come up with two ways to show it to readers (focus on different elements of it). You want the hero to fail, so make him fail miserably. Or at least make it memorable for readers. This reversal sets up the finale; what isn't accomplished here will be accomplished there, so make it count.

The hero's wife is cheating on him? Okay … but with whom? How does he find out? Are other people there to witness his humiliation? Does it cost him anything else, like a job, when people find out? How does the wife react? Does she tell him she never loved him? And most importantly, why does it matter? There are so many options, so many things to consider here. Make sure you are considering everything about your reversal so that it is the best it can be.

Write down your reversal as it is right now, then add more depth to it.

REVERSAL BRAINSTORM

CURRENT REVERSAL

	How This Would Alter the Current Reversal
New Information	
New Situation	
Unexpected Betrayals	
Unexpected Shows of Support	
Last-Minute Change of Plans	
Change of Heart	
Change in Perceptions	

Is one way to alter a reversal better than another? Did any new ideas pop up? Play with this a bit. Keep digging for the one piece of detail that brings this reversal to life. Who? What? When? Where? Why? All of these can be considered—try the reversal from every possible permutation or angle.

CHECK YOUR PACING

Pacing in fiction refers to how quickly events unfold. Since pacing is one of the most difficult things to fix in the rewrite stage, it helps to think about it a bit now. Pacing usually comes into play around the middle of the story, because things tend to quicken as you start to near the ending. Pacing can be manipulated if you:

- use shorter sentences;
- use shorter paragraphs;
- start in the midst of the action;
- add a time element, like a timer counting down;
- have one-word dialogues between characters;
- cut from one action to the middle of another one;
- keep exposition brief and to the point; and
- use cliffhangers, as we discussed on Day 10.

Pacing is a very subjective and intuitive thing. You just have to feel your way around it. You don't want to stop your 30-day progress to worry too much about it, but just keep it in mind so you don't wind up giving yourself too much to do in the rewrite stage. This is why it is important to have an outline of some type; it helps you address such concerns.

The best way to learn about pacing is to read tons of books in your favorite genre. Learn how the pros do it. You may struggle with it a bit in the beginning of your career, but it gets easier and easier with each story you write.

DAY 18

I want to do it because I want to do it.

—Amelia Earhart

OBJECTIVES

• Perform a genre status check to see if you have enough elements to qualify for your genre.

• Make sure you are conveying the right information to readers.

CONDUCT A GENRE STATUS CHECK

This is the second half of Week 3. Let's make sure that you are on track and that your manuscript is living up to the standards established by the genre in which you're writing. Use the Genre Elements Tracker on page 176 to make sure your story is up to par. You can't sell a mystery if there is nothing mysterious about it. Here's a quick list of unique elements to include for various genres:

• **Mystery:** Include red herrings or clues.

• **Romance:** Include love or delayed-love scene.

• **Erotica:** Include erotic scenes.

• **Drama:** Include dark moments.

• **Horror:** Include scary (sometimes gory) events.

• **Suspense:** Include cliffhangers.

• **Comedy:** Include funny moments.

- **Chick-Lit:** Include quirky moments (possibly those revelations that make the main character seem like a real, everyday woman).

- **Anti-Plot Fiction:** Include subversive moments. (Read *Story Structure Architect* for more about this complicated genre. Many non-Westerners like this style.)

- **True-Life Stories:** Include moments that are unusual, revealing, enlightening, or shocking.

- **Literary Fiction:** Include incidents that portray your purpose for writing this story. If you want to show how a man's life can easily fall apart, then have three good examples that convey this.

We are not talking about craft and creativity here; we are talking about basic genre elements. Sometimes during the writing process, it is easy to forget that your book needs to have at least three examples of how it fits genre conventions.

Sometimes it is just a case of being so close to your work that you can't tell you are missing these elements, or you are just writing so fast you forget to make sure you are on track regarding genre. After all, you do not want to be in the romance section if your book doesn't have much romance in it. You will lose all your readers.

The following Genre Elements Tracker helps you make sure you are meeting the minimum requirements for your genre. It also helps you see how these elements work together and build as the story progresses. It may even help you design your ending.

If you already have more than three genre elements, which is great, then list the three main elements. They are usually the ones that move the story forward or push it in a new direction the most.

In *Casablanca*, there are several dark moments to show readers this is a drama—Rick's past haunts him and has made him seem heartless. In *Dracula*, there are several scary moments to show readers this is horror—blood, insanity, and death abound. Could you imagine finding *Casablanca* in the horror section? Or *Dracula* in the comedy section? We waited until Week 3 to explore this because you were busy creating your story foundation in Weeks 1 and 2, and you needed to get to know the characters a bit. If you find you don't have genre elements in Act I, just jot down what you think should be there and then mark it on your notes sheet for the rewrite. The same rules apply—don't stop to rewrite anything just yet. Jot it down on your Story Tracker sheet and keep moving forward as if you've made those changes.

If you don't see any genre elements in Act II, then look over the scenes you will write in the next few days and rework one so it fulfills a genre element.

Act III hasn't been written yet, so you are free to add and delete these elements as necessary. It is always great if the finale pays off for your genre. This means that, if you are writing a romance, your readers would love to have the entire romance paid off in the finale or the resolution after the finale—the hero defeats the villain and then marries the heroine. He won't defeat the villain and then *leave* the heroine … unless this is a drama.

GENRE ELEMENTS TRACKER

ACT I	ACT II	ACT III
Element	**Element**	**Element**
Characters	**Characters**	**Characters**
Props or Items Used	**Props or Items Used**	**Props or Items Used**
Intended Reader Response	**Intended Reader Response**	**Intended Reader Response**
Other Notes	**Other Notes**	**Other Notes**

DAY 19

Any activity becomes creative when the doer cares about doing it right, or better.

—John Updike

OBJECTIVES

- Identify your golden writing hours so you know when you are most creative.

- Complete the Villain Brainstorm, because a strong villain makes for a strong finale.

IDENTIFY YOUR GOLDEN HOURS

By Week 3, you should have a feel for when your best writing time is. It's important to identify your peak performance hours, because while you may not have the luxury of always writing at that particular time, you know that when you do, it's likely to be especially rewarding. Pinpoint your golden hours by considering the following:

- Do you find yourself writing or thinking about your project in the morning? Afternoon? Night?

- Do you find it is easier for you to get into your creative zone at certain times of the day?

- If you can't identify a set time of day when it seems to be easier for you to write, consider other potential factors. Are you calmer or happier after certain activities, like yoga or running? Do you think clearer when the kids are asleep or your spouse is out?

- Is there something you do differently during those golden hours that you could start doing during your allotted writing time?

Once you've identified a specific time period or a certain set of circumstances that seem to heighten your creative energy, try to recreate such circumstances to suit your writing needs. This way, you can bring your golden hours with you. One writer I know felt very creative just before going to bed. She started writing down her routine and found that she listened to classical music at night just before sleep. She started listening to this music during her writing time, which was after lunch, and recaptured that creative feeling.

Think about how you feel during the hours of a usual weekday. Include anything that may be affecting your moods or any major responsibilities you have that can't be changed. Jot down what you have learned in these three weeks about your most productive writing time. Be honest.

We all have peaks and valleys in every area of life. Ideally, you should be able to write anytime, anywhere—that is what professional writers do. They don't wait for the muse, and neither should you. But if you can utilize your best hours, things might flow a little easier in the beginning for you.

DEVELOP YOUR VILLAIN

How is your villain doing? He helps initiate the story in Act I, then he usually takes a backseat while the main characters take over a bit in Act II. But right about now is when he needs to come back onto the scene full force. He needs to create more tension to push the hero toward the finale.

Many writers think it takes more creativity to create a great villain than it does to create a great hero. This may be true. We love our heroes and know them all too well. Since we don't like to make things hard on our beloved characters, we tend to dislike the villain and certainly have a hard time making him a strong adversary. But think of it this way: how can your hero shine if the villain is weak or one-dimensional? Your hero needs a strong villain.

Now that you are nearing the end of Act II, Part 2, you need to think a bit about how the villain will help the hero shine in Act III. Even if your hero will be defeated in the end, the hero should still remain sympathetic and likable, someone readers feel for. And our perception of the hero is always colored—sometimes subtly, sometimes in broad strokes—by our perception of the villain.

First, your villain needs some redeeming qualities. He may be bad, but he usually has a reason for being bad; perhaps he has been victimized himself. Indeed, he may truly believe he is being *good*; think of the religious zealot who believes he has to kill someone to save or "purify" him.

Second, your villain needs a skill that equals or surpasses the hero's skill in some way. This skill can be different from what the hero can do, but just as powerful. We usually don't get to see it until near the end of Act III. This way, the stakes are made higher in the moments before the final confrontation.

Third, your villain needs a weakness that can be exploited in the finale. You also need to find a way to let the hero find out about this weakness. If possible, your villain should also find out about the hero's weakness in the finale but be unable to defeat the hero.

VILLAIN BRAINSTORM

Redeeming Qualities	Skills	Weaknesses

I hope this helps spark some more ideas about the big finale! That's
what these quick worksheets are for—to help you make quick decisions
so your story is on track while keeping you from getting distracted
with overanalysis.

DAY 20

Do not bother just to be better than your contemporaries or predecessors.
Try to be better than yourself.

—WILLIAM FAULKNER

OBJECTIVES

- Develop your Act II turning point so you can set up the final confrontation.

- Figure out your hero's story compass so you know where your hero—and your story—is headed.

DEVELOP YOUR ACT II TURNING POINT

By the end of this week, you should be working on your second turning point. This turning point turns the plot and characters toward the finale. It propels the entire ending, so make it count. The one difference is that the main character is usually forced into making a decision that propels this turning point (thus the reversal). This way, he actively creates the events of the story and gets involved in setting up the final climax. In novels, this means getting 75 percent or so of the book completed.

Look back at your At-A-Glance Outline from Day 3 and state your Act II turning point here:

ACT II TURNING POINT

_____

Brainstorm a bit to see if there are any other ideas you can use, any other directions you can go in, or different character reactions to this turning point that could spice it up. Play with it a bit to see if it brings up any possibilities.

ACT II TURNING POINT BRAINSTORM

What is the exact opposite that could happen at this turning point?

What is the most outrageous thing that could happen at this point?

What would happen if you brought in another character?

How do you want readers to react or feel at this point?

CHART YOUR HERO'S PATH

In which direction will your hero and story travel toward the finale? You are about to finish up Act II and race through Act III, so now is a great time to think about this. It can also be frustrating to come to the finale and not have a real plan in place. Let's take a look at your hero's options. He can:

- obtain his goal;
- abandon his goal for a new one;
- try but fail to achieve his goal; or
- give up.

Each direction on the story compass below says something different about the hero, plot, and theme. In the end, do you want your hero to succeed or fail? How much will he succeed—does he succeed in the fact that he tried (but failed), or does he completely obtain his goal as he imagined it? Will the hero decide that the goal is not worth obtaining anymore, that something else is more important? (He wants more time with his family, for example.)

Go ahead and brainstorm different outcomes for each of the possible options on the following story compass, and think about which one works best with the story you've drafted. You might find it helpful to take a look back at your At-A-Glance Outline from Day 3 to make sure the options you come up with are in line with your original vision for your story's climax.

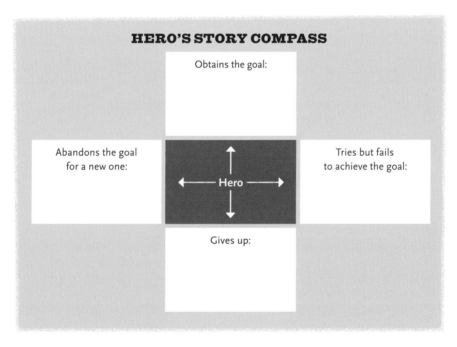

Now you have the finale in mind and know what direction you are going in for Week 4. Most likely, the hero will succeed, so you are setting up this turning point to lead the hero to success.

Keep in mind that in Acts I and II, you want to plant anything you need to that will help the hero succeed (or fail) in Act III—just don't make things too obvious for readers. It can be a subtle clue, or maybe a small prop that will help the hero succeed in the end. Readers shouldn't really notice it until it comes up later, but they should remember it once it comes up again: "Oh, that's right, the heroine left a gun in her purse four chapters ago, so when the hero sees her purse sitting there, he knows there's a gun in it." You are foreshadowing something that will help the hero succeed (or fail) in the finale.

Why are you thinking about this at the end of Act II? Because you want to set it up far enough in advance so readers don't feel like you are just throwing the ending together in the final act. It helps build believability if the finale is slowly set up at this point instead of in the last few pages.

Another word of caution here: Don't use the "hand of God" technique. This is when you have some unusual thing happen to save the day—a new character comes out of nowhere and hands the hero the money he needs, or a storm blows in and kills the villain for the heroine (this is also called a *deus ex machina*). Make sure you are leading toward an ending that is organic to the story. Set it up now so that you will have something believable later on.

DAY 21

Every day, in every way, I am getting better and better.
— Émile Coué

OBJECTIVES

• Keep writing—you need to wrap up Act II by the end of the week.

• Keep your hero motivated by dangling believable rewards.

KEEP WRITING

Keep on writing today. Make sure you are on schedule and meeting your weekly goals. If any of the worksheets are confusing you or making you doubt your story, then, again, set them aside for the rewrite and keep moving forward. Forward momentum is the most important thing right now … and, as we approach Act III, your forward momentum should be picking up even more speed.

This is it, the end of Week 3! Wow, you have come a long way. I'm sure you have written more than you thought possible. Even if you stopped here, you should feel a sense of accomplishment. Three weeks of writing almost every day—or even just three weeks of meeting your personal writing goals—is huge! You know you can make this a habit, a big part of your life now. See the good that you have done; don't focus on the mistakes or setbacks. Stay positive!

KEEP YOUR HERO MOTIVATED

As you move closer to Act III, you may want to have your hero get a glance at his reward to remind him why he is doing this. Let him see what he will gain from the coming finale if he succeeds (though he may not succeed; that's up to you). Don't make it too obvious. If he is going to win a thousand dollars, you don't have to show him a billboard covered in dollar signs. Try to be more subtle than that; simply having him watch a person of wealth getting into and driving away in his Ferrari will make the point, for the character as well as for readers.

Think about your own goals in life. Aren't there some coincidences that happen almost daily to remind you of your goals, as if the universe were pushing you along? Maybe you are out having lunch and the woman at the table next to you starts talking about how she just started her new business and is so happy. Now you remember you said you were going to start a small cookie business this summer, and you know it will make you happy, too.

Give your hero the same type of nudge at some point in Act II. Reaffirm his goal and his potential reward. This will reaffirm it for the reader as well. However, make sure that how you choose to nudge your character is in line with the rest of your story and with your characterization. Take a look back at your At-A-Glance Outline from Day 3 and your Hero's Story Compass from Day 20. Consider the obstacles he's already overcome, as well as the ones still to come, and brainstorm what it will take to keep your hero motivated through Act III.

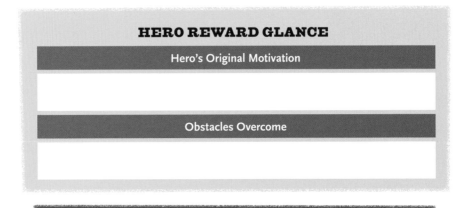

HERO REWARD GLANCE

Hero's Original Motivation

Obstacles Overcome

Obstacles Still to Come

Intended Story Resolution

Reward Options

1.

2.

3.

WEEK 3 WRAP-UP

Congratulations! This is the end of the third week.

- Are you saying the Week 3 mantra every day?

- Are you sticking to the five secrets and not rewriting while as you go?

- How did the Theme Spider worksheet turn out? You'll be doing more theme work next week, so don't shrug this one off!

- Do you have at least three genre-specific elements in your story?

- Was a scene sequence necessary? If so, how does it help your story?

- Have you kept a list of things you need to research later on? Review them now.

- Are you portraying your villain as a three-dimensional opponent?

- Did you nudge your hero in the right direction?

PROGRESS TRACKER

Week 1: 25%	Week 2: 50%	Week 3: 75%	Week 4: 100%

Welcome to Week 4! This is it—the finish line is in sight. Just seven days left to reach your goal and get that manuscript completed. This week focuses on writing the final obstacle, the climax, and the resolution. You will finish the final quarter of your manuscript. Doesn't it feel wonderful?

Okay, okay ... maybe it has been an *intense* three weeks thus far, and I know a lot of inner issues come up for anyone who tries to reach for her goal, no matter what that goal is. That is why the first half of the book addresses these issues head on: Writing a book—in a month or otherwise—is not just about prose work, but about personal work. It requires an enormous investment in and of yourself, and not just in terms of time. It requires you to look deep within yourself to find out what you're made of, which can be a frightening, frustrating, and difficult process. But that's exactly what makes it a valuable one: You're about to come out of this not only with a book in your hands, but with the knowledge that you pushed yourself to achieve something special.

So don't let resistance, fatigue, jitters, or *anything else* undo all the work you've already done ... keep writing! Put your butt in the chair and get to work.

TRADITIONAL STORY STRUCTURE: ACT III

In Act II, our hero enjoyed what looked to be a triumph; then, the situation reversed and led to the darkest moment yet for the hero and/or for those around him—by all accounts, a point of no return. But, in truth, this was not point of no return at all; rather, it was Act II's crucial turning point, leading the hero toward a final showdown with the villain and leading us to Act III. But there's still one thing standing in our hero's way before he can confront the villain, one last obstacle he must face in order to earn the right to face the villain and, hopefully, resolve the conflict once and for all.

• **Final Obstacle:** The main character is forced, through the momentum of the turning point, to face one last huge obstacle. He is pushed to the limit not just physically, but mentally and emotionally as well. Here are some things to think about for your final obstacle:

- If the main character is going to be successful, this is where he sets up the villain to be destroyed.

- If the main character is going to be defeated, this is where he is set up for the villain to come in and do away with him.

- If the main character is going to abandon his goal, this is where he tries to achieve a new goal.

CASABLANCA

Rick arranges the meeting between himself, Laszlo, and Ilsa intended to set Laszlo up to take a fall. When they arrive at his club, Rick hands over the letters of transit, at which time Louis steps out of the shadows to make the arrest, gloating that Rick has sold Laszlo out for love. But when Louis turns to face Rick, he finds that he is facing instead the barrel of a gun; Rick has turned the tables. He orders Louis to call the airport to secure safe passage on a plane out of Casablanca, but Louis instead calls Strasser, the Nazi commander, to tip him off. At the airport, Rick makes Louis fill out the letters of transit ... in the names of Mr. and Mrs. Victor Laszlo. Despite his love for Ilsa and his own need for happiness, he realizes that there are some things in life bigger than his own needs and wants; he is willing to sacrifice his happiness for Ilsa's, and for her safety. He has faced this final obstacle, an internal one, and set himself up for success in the end, though "success" means that he will never again see the love of his life.

DRACULA

The final obstacles faced by Harker and his men are those of distance and time, as they race across Eastern Europe toward the difficult terrain of Transylvania in pursuit of the Count and the gypsies in his service. The men realize they are headed into the heart of the Count's territory, his homeland, but they also realize that any chance for success, any chance to save Mina's life, rests with confronting and finishing him.

- **Climax:** The main character comes face to face with the villain. The problem is either resolved and the goal is accomplished, or vice versa.

CASABLANCA

The Laszlos board the plane as Strasser arrives. Strasser has one last chance to prevent the plane from taking off and picks up the phone to radio the tower, determined to capture Laszlo. But Rick isn't prepared to let that happen; he pulls out his gun and warns Strasser, and when Strasser refuses to lower the phone, Rick shoots him. The police arrive as the plane carrying the Laszlos safely lifts off.

DRACULA

The Count makes it to the castle, but Van Helsing has arrived beforehand and sealed the entrances with sacred objects. Weakened and unable to find solace inside the castle, the Count faces Harker and his men for one final showdown. The men prevail and the Count is slain, releasing Mina from the vampire's curse.

• **Resolution:** All loose ends are tied up. All subplots are resolved, and the main character reflects on the events of the story. Has he changed at all? How has the story affected him? What are his attitudes about the events he just went through?

CASABLANCA

Rick stares at Louis, wondering if he is to be arrested for aiding Laszlo and killing Strasser. Instead, Louis tells his men to round up "the usual suspects," and he walks off with Rick, marking the beginning of a "beautiful friendship." More importantly, Rick has come full circle from the beginning, from a man who sticks his neck out "for no one" to one capable of self-sacrifice and companionship.

DRACULA

In a flash-forward we see Mina, Harker, and their young son enjoying their lives together, realizing the happiness that is now theirs to be "well worth the pain they endured." These characters have come full circle, and when they recall the horrific events they witnessed and endured, seven years past, they do so now "without despair."

DAY 22

The difference between perseverance and obstinacy is that one often comes from a strong will, and the other from a strong won't.

—HENRY WARD BEECHER

OBJECTIVES

• Identify your Week 4 goal, because this week can be the hardest one to stay focused in. If you need to deviate from the outlined BIAM plan for whatever reason, today's the day to map out your week.

• Make sure your villain is up the challenge presented in the final act by evaluating his motivation. Complete the Villain Reward Glance to make sure his goals are solid.

IDENTIFY YOUR WEEK 4 GOAL

What are your goals for the fourth week? If you are way behind, adjust your goals and get yourself ready for the next month. (Remember, you can customize the BIAM calendar if you find that you've fallen behind—don't give up!) Spend the fourth week preparing your story and going over that outline if you need to regroup for next time.

If you are right on track, and hopefully you are, finish that ending. Get Act III down. Even if you come up a bit short in word or page count, get to those final words: "The End." Take as much time and care as you can. You want to make this count. The ending has to pay off for readers. A great story can be ruined if you leave readers with questions or don't pay off all the promises you made in the first three acts. (All readers will remember is the unfulfilling ending, not the amazing beginning.) The great beginning keeps them reading this book, but a great ending keeps them thinking about it long after they've put the book down.

At the very least, you must make sure you pay off the genre you are writing for. In a romance, the hero and heroine must get together in the end, and in a mystery, the crime must be solved; otherwise, you are not writing for these genres.

Don't be afraid to finish the story and let it go, either. Too many writers get one story in their minds, work on it for years and years, and never let it go. Their whole career becomes a memorial for this one story, this one character. It becomes like a security blanket. As long as they continue to work on it, no one can judge it, no one can reject it. They feel as if they will lose their whole writing career if they fail with this one story, because they have put so much into it. Nonsense! If this is you, write an outline for your next story right away! Then you will feel safer about finishing this one and letting it go. Endings bring up all these issues. Just remember that you will have other story ideas to write about; you are not a one-hit wonder. You will create other interesting characters. You may even look back years from now and think your best work is still ahead of you. Writing the ending is all part of the letting go process. You need to have closure with this story so you can rewrite, send it out there, and move on to the next idea.

KEEP YOUR VILLAIN MOTIVATED

Just as you did a Reward Glance sheet for your hero, you should also do one for your villain. The stronger his desire for his goal, the more he will fight against the hero. The key here is to make sure the villain's goal is in direct conflict with the hero's goal. It's as if the villain's goal forces him to make sure the hero's goal does not happen. They come into direct conflict with each other.

CASABLANCA

Strasser and the Nazis want Laszlo arrested and want to take possession of the stolen letters of transit. Louis, as prefect of Casablanca, feels compelled to aid them (not to mention, he sees the potential for personal advancement in doing so). Laszlo wants the letters so that he can escape to America, taking his wife—Rick's true love—with him. *All* are villains or antagonists in the story, though coming from very different motivations and perspectives, and all push Rick to make a choice in the end.

DRACULA

The Count wants Mina to be his bride, but Harker wants Mina to be his bride as well. This story is an interesting example in that both the hero and the villain are motivated by a seemingly positive force: love. It might even be tempting to call the Count the hero of the story because of this; the Count's goal is to be reunited with his long-lost wife, who he believes is reincarnated in Mina. But his method for doing so is to make Mina a vampire, condemning her to eternal life, and so Harker knows he can only reach *his* goal—to save Mina and live happily with her—if he kills the Count.

What is *your* villain's goal, and how does it come into conflict with the hero's goal? Why does the villain want this goal? Take a look at your At-A-Glance Outline from Day 3, your Hero Reward Glance from Day 21, and your Villain Brainstorm from Day 19. Brainstorm some possible reward scenarios to keep your villain motivated enough to give it his all in the upcoming climactic scene.

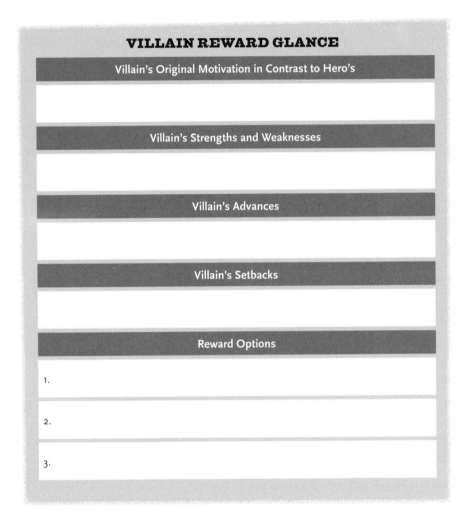

VILLAIN REWARD GLANCE

Villain's Original Motivation in Contrast to Hero's

Villain's Strengths and Weaknesses

Villain's Advances

Villain's Setbacks

Reward Options
1.
2.
3.

A truly well-written villain makes the hero push himself to reach his goal or work even harder to become a better person. It's almost as if the villain is the hero's teacher. In life, we usually learn more when we butt heads with someone than if we only meet nice, happy people who don't challenge us.

There's an old story about an angry, unpleasant old man who moves near a monastery, and the monks, bothered by this, ask their teacher to make the man move. The teacher simply replies, "It is the greatest master who can leave the monastery and live masterfully among the people. Perhaps I will invite him to dinner." In other words, this angry old man is the best teacher the monks could ask for; who better to teach them about patience and calm abiding? The same is true for your villain. It's the adversity brought on by your villain that reveals your hero for who he truly is.

Perhaps your villain could also aggravate a personality flaw in the hero that he needs to heal. Villains can symbolize the dark, hidden, shadow side of the hero that he has been trying to suppress.

DAY 23

We were born to succeed, not to fail.

—HENRY DAVID THOREAU

OBJECTIVE

- Check your character arc so you can really make the ending all it can be.

CHART YOUR CHARACTER ARC

Go over your character worksheets from Days 4, 6, 9, 12, 20, and 21. Your hero has come along way since those early days! It's time to make sure he can go the last mile. To do this, you've got to look at who your character is at the start of your story and chart how the events of your storyline—all the character's successes, setbacks, and failures—have changed him on the inside. Can you see the character arc progressing through your story acts? Fill out the Character Arc Tracker and get a feel for how the story's significant events have affected your character.

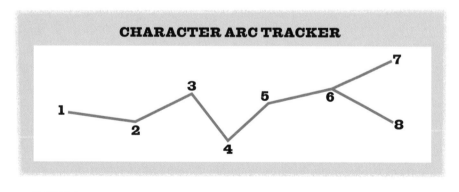

1. Your character at the start of Act I:	2. Your character at the Act I turning point:	3. Your character at the Act I temporary triumph:	4. Your character at the Act I reversal:
5. Your character at the Act II temporary triumph:	6. Your character at the Act III climax:	7. Your character succeeds:	8. Your character fails:

Now that you've mapped out your hero's journey over the course of your story, it's time to think about how you convey your character's transformation to readers in Act III:

How will you signify the hero's transformation?

Another important question to consider is how your other characters are going to react to your hero's evolution. In real life, we lose friends all the time because we have outgrown them or just drifted apart. There are so many different ways that people and their relationships with each other can change, and, as the writer, you need to examine more than one way the members of your supporting cast will react to your transformed hero:

How will other characters deal with the hero's character arc at the end of your story? (This can be part of your story's resolution.)

These reactions make it all the more real for the hero as well as the readers. Everything we do in life has consequences, even growing as a person and bettering ourselves. Hey, you can't become a positive, loving person if you surround yourself with negative, angry people! At least, it makes the journey much harder than it has to be.

This is why you will see many characters feeling like they need to get away from home in order to find themselves, or why you see so many coming-of-age stories that take place at college. The main character needs to be on his own to grow and change, away from the influence of his family or community. If your spouse came home and said, "I quit my job to be a clown full time," you might lose it. But if you are on a first date with someone who works as a clown, you might not be so upset about it. You don't have a long history with this person or the expectations that go with it.

DAY 24

Whatever you vividly imagine, ardently desire, sincerely believe,
and enthusiastically act upon ... must inevitably come to pass!
—PAUL J. MEYER

OBJECTIVES

• Develop your story's crucial final obstacle.

• Craft a dynamic climax.

By the end of this week, you should be working on your final obstacle
and climax. But even if you feel slightly out of steam at this point—and
granted, you've been working your hardest for almost a full month
now—remember two things: First, these are the crucial moments you've
been writing toward all along. Maybe these were even the first scenes
that came to mind when the idea revealed itself to you. Remember how
excited you felt when considering the heroine, having faced all the ups
and downs of her journey, finally coming to the climactic scenes where
she faces down the villain (and her own shortcomings) to succeed? Can
you recall the exhilaration you felt the last time you read a good book
and these key moments began to build? The final obstacle and climax
require, and should be full of, *energy* ... as pure and kinetic as you can
put on the page. This is what you've been working toward these last few
weeks, and what your readers have been looking forward to. You've done
a lot of meticulous work so that, now, you can play. Have fun! Enjoy it!
Raise your energy to a fever pitch, and the energy on the page will follow.

Oh, and that second thing to keep in mind: After the final obstacle
and the climax, all that remains to write is the resolution, a very short

scene that serves to tie up all loose ends and to bring your story to a satisfying final impression. You're almost at the finish line; put your head down, keep your feet moving, and reach deep to find that extra bit of strength and stamina you need.

DEVELOP YOUR FINAL OBSTACLE

The final obstacle is the point where the hero's faith, resolve, character, or endurance is put to one final test before the *true* test—the conflict with the villain—comes about. It is also, then, the setup for your climax, so you want to make sure that this obstacle: (1) makes sense according to what you've established in the story, i.e., that your final obstacle isn't a giant lizard creature that drops from the sky, especially if you've been writing a mystery; and (2) reveals something of what's ultimately at stake in the climax. It's the bridge, in other words, between all that's come before and the important thing that lies ahead. So let's make it a good one.

First, write the final obstacle description you developed as part of your outline back on Day 3:

FINAL OBSTACLE

In all likelihood, your description is a little vague, a little general—you were only outlining, after all. The Hero's Story Compass from Day 20 and the Character Arc Tracker from Day 23 will both come in handy here as you flesh out your final obstacle and make sure it aligns with how you want your story to end and your hero's intended character arc. As you brainstorm different final obstacle possibilities, remember to consider how they'll influence your climactic scene.

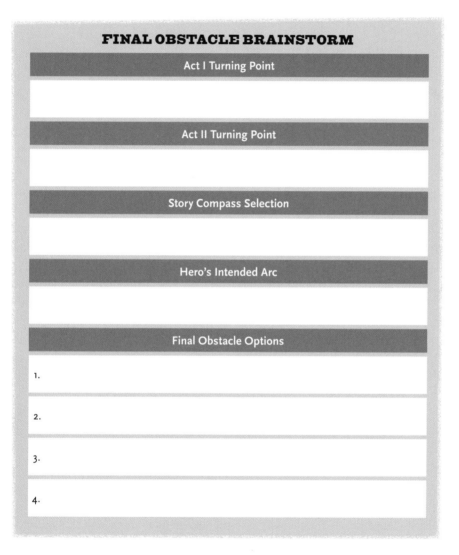

FINAL OBSTACLE BRAINSTORM

Act I Turning Point

Act II Turning Point

Story Compass Selection

Hero's Intended Arc

Final Obstacle Options
1.
2.
3.
4.

Did you account for everything? Are you using the main character's strengths and weaknesses? How does the villain factor in? Are you setting up the climax? Are you using the setting, or possibly subplots, to move it forward? Can you make it more challenging?

Consider all these questions. Now is the time to bring everything out in the open. The hero is facing his final test regarding his new character arc. Will he grow and change? Does he seem ready to face and hopefully defeat the villain to reach his goal? Try to get readers to question whether this will happen. Build tension and suspense as much as you can. Raise the stakes for the final conflict. The best way to do this is to make the villain stronger or somehow stack the deck against the hero. Don't be afraid to make things tough for him.

CRAFT YOUR CLIMAX

Finally, after all the twists and turns of your book, this is where your main character comes face to face with the villain and where the problem is either resolved and the goal is accomplished, or vice versa. This element is usually quick and fast-paced … and you've likely had it in your head for a while, if not all along. Take a look at the climax you wrote for your Day 3 outline:

CLIMAX

How does it look now that you've drafted the first two acts of your story and are closing in on the final scenes? Is your climax the best it can be? Is it different from what has been done before not only in this story, but also in this genre? Brainstorm your climax to explore more options.

CLIMAX BRAINSTORM

Final Obstacle Recap

Characters

Setting and Props

Genre Considerations

Climax Options
1.
2.
3.
4.

Did you set up the climax well? Is there anything else you can add to really get readers interested? Can you up the stakes even more? Is it organic to the story? (Make sure elements do not come out of nowhere;

remember our earlier discussion of verisimilitude. If your final conflict takes place in the desert, you're not going to defeat the villain by throwing nearby snowballs.)

If the main character uses a special skill to defeat the villain, then make sure to jot that down on your notes sheet so you can foreshadow it in the beginning. Once you get to the climax, you may find you have a lot you need to go back and set up to make the climax believable. That's okay. That's what the notes sheet is for.

We all know that in a romance the hero will rescue the heroine, or the heroine the hero, but try to make it different from all the other romances out there. Strive to find one interesting twist you can add to your ending so this book stands out. Who knows? Maybe you will find a moment of *comedy* you can add to spice it up. You can always change it later in the rewrite, so don't censor or second-guess yourself too much now. Find the momentum of the scene and follow it. The particulars can be tweaked as you need, but finding the right tone or energy to propel readers to—and through—the climax is important. More than that, though, it should be a lot of fun not only for readers to read, but also for you, the writer, to write.

DAY 25

Throughout the centuries there were men who took first steps down new roads armed with nothing but their own vision.

—Ayn Rand

OBJECTIVES

• Complete the Theme Revelation Check.

• Write the resolution so you can tie up all loose ends.

FULLY REVEAL YOUR THEME

Before you write the resolution, the final piece of your story, make sure you have paid off the theme. If you haven't, then you need to be prepared to work it into your resolution. This is where most themes are paid off. Keep in mind, though, this payoff is very, very subtle. This is why each reader may have a slightly different take on what the theme of a story is. Its subtlety allows for different interpretations, as seen in the *Casablanca* and *Dracula* examples.

CASABLANCA

You have to confront your past to change your future. Or, you have to be willing to sacrifice a part of yourself to fully find yourself. Or, if you love somebody, set them free.

The mysterious, ancient world has terrors the modern, industrialized world doesn't fully understand. Or, sex is violence and turns chastity (*female* chastity) into bloodlust. Or, if you love somebody, keep them close.

All of the themes just mentioned for *Casablanca* and *Dracula* are present because the authors worked them—both consciously and unconsciously—in their stories. The themes aren't developed by readers, but readers are able to independently interpret the themes as we've just done. So what themes have you been working with in *yours*?

Look back at the basic theme concept you developed for your Day 3 outline, as well as at the Theme Spider you did on Day 15. What did you come up with? Have you hinted at your theme throughout your story? Make notes of any symbols, motifs, or metaphors you need to plug into the story to reinforce your thematic message ... and any you found yourself working with that might have surprised you.

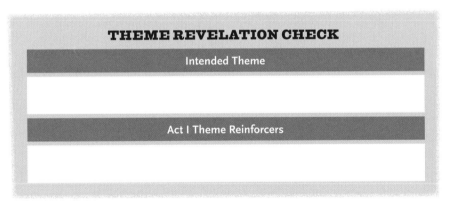

THEME REVELATION CHECK

Intended Theme

Act I Theme Reinforcers

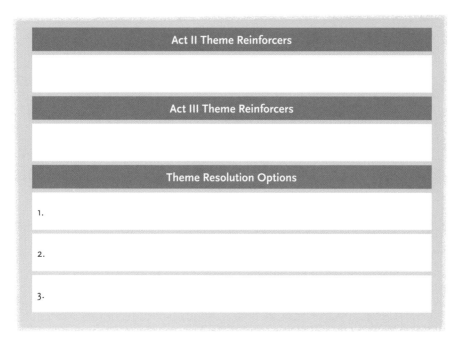

Act II Theme Reinforcers

Act III Theme Reinforcers

Theme Resolution Options
1.
2.
3.

DRAFT YOUR RESOLUTION

The resolution is the final piece of the plot puzzle. The hero has faced the villain, and he can now take a breather. All of the subplots need to be resolved now, and you should leave readers with a sense of what the hero's life will be like from here on out. Consider the following questions as you prepare to write your resolution:

- How will the hero's world be different?

- Will things will be better? Worse?

- Has a new problem briefly presented itself, hinting at a possible sequel?

- Have the secondary characters made their feelings known regarding the changes in the hero? How might they, and what will the feelings be?

- Is there some detail or motif from the beginning that might be mirrored in the resolution for a bit of closure? (For instance, a dog walked by in the opening and now here he is again—perhaps as a symbol for something else.)

Remember to keep the tone of the resolution consistent with the rest of the story—you certainly don't see a comedic resolution at the end of *Dracula*. It would confuse readers after such heavy material and thus cheapen what's come before it.

Remember, too, that you're resolving three things here: (1) your main storyline, (2) all the subplots, and (3) the character arc. You don't want any loose ends. Take a few minutes now to brainstorm resolutions for each of the points identified above. And be sure that the endings you provide complement one another.

RESOLUTION BRAINSTORM

Plot Resolution	Subplot Resolution	Character Resolution

DAY 26

> Write while the heat is in you. The writer who postpones the recording of his thoughts uses an iron which has cooled to burn a hole with. He cannot inflame the minds of his audience.
>
> —Henry David Thoreau

OBJECTIVES

- Keep writing.

- Make sure your story lives up to its promise.

KEEP WRITING

You only have a few days left. Don't worry about how much you have or have not reached your goal. Just push yourself to keep moving forward. There is always *next* month, after all, but you'll want to get as much done as possible right now. You can do it. Many other writers before have done it. It is possible to write a book in a month. Don't give up.

VERIFY YOUR STORY PROMISE

What did you promise your readers on the first page? Besides the genre elements, what do your readers expect to get from this story after reading the first page or first chapter? If you've written a mystery, we know to expect some conundrum for the main character to figure out, but what *else* is promised up front? Something unique to your book, something uniquely yours? Janet Evanovich usually promises some fun through comedy and quirky characters. Stephen King usually promises some interesting details to keep your imagination running wild at night. Barbara G. Walker opens her novel *Amazon* with this: "Under the Goddess-given laws of my motherclan, a warrior woman was not allowed to choose a husband and bear children until she had achieved her first kill in battle." What does this promise? It is a bit shocking, as we are used to hearing such things of male characters. So this book promises to completely upset our ideas of gender. It promises the portrayal of tough women; no glamour here, just raw feminist themes with a touch of female-centric religion to boot.

Now look back at your opening image or hook—what does *it* promise? What promises do you make in your first page or chapter that should be fulfilled by the novel's end and might even make a reappearance in the resolution?

STORY PROMISES
_____

Can you connect your ending to that promise? Can you take some of those elements and visit them again in the climax or resolution? In *Casablanca*, Rick is at the airport with the letters of transit that opened the film, and he is helping desperate people—the Laszlos—escape. In *Dracula*, the Count travels back to his castle—the same place where the story began—allowing the closing scene to mirror the opening one.

STORY PROMISE CONNECTIONS
_____

DAY 27

Failure is the path of least persistence.

—ANONYMOUS

OBJECTIVE

- Check your progress. After all, there's nothing like a close look at how far you've come to help you go the last few miles.

CHECK YOUR PROGRESS

Let's take a moment to figure out just how far you have come during this process. What did you get from the journey? Remember how we discussed resistance? If a refresher is needed, you may want to go back and re-read that chapter now.

Most BIAMers lose steam in Week 4 ... *most*. If that is not you, then *wonderful!* Just indulge me a bit. (Maybe you can apply the following to another, non-writing-related goal.)

You should feel something like this when you are nearing the end: excited, happy, energized, relieved. But you may find yourself feeling this way instead: frustrated, anxious, rushed, overwhelmed. If this is the case, then you may just have a block surfacing. Sometimes the inner critic rears his ugly head at this stage. As we move toward our goals, feelings of low self-esteem or self-worth may arise. Recognize that this is happening. Be self-aware. Notice that you are feeling this way and then keep moving forward in spite of it.

You are just trying to stop yourself because you're afraid that you'll:

- succeed and have to work long hours from now on in order to maintain that same level of success;

- fail and lose your dream of being a famous writer;

- have to sell out to really get published;

- have to let go of your characters and story because "What if you're a one-hit wonder?"; or

- overshadow a friend who always wanted to be a writer but who has never been able to finish anything.

But if you don't finish this manuscript, your fears will become reality. Write down why you secretly don't want to finish this book. Then write down the truth—why this fear is false. (Those of you who are excited and energized can skip this one exercise.)

WHY I DON'T WANT TO FINISH

THE TRUTH BEHIND MY FEAR

Remember that this is a learning process. It is not just about writing a book in a month. You are learning a lot about yourself and about your life. Making room for something new, for changes, can bring up some issues for you. But that's what makes the work important and valuable.

DAY 28

Write only if you cannot live without writing. Write only what you alone can write.

—ELIE WIESEL

OBJECTIVE

• Complete the Final Story Check worksheet to fill in any last holes and to get a feel for your overall finished story.

FIND AND FILL STORY HOLES

Read through your pages for the week and check to see if there are any holes—you should be skilled at this by now. Jot down any observations on your notes and research sheets. Sometimes we want to make up for the lack of tension and drama that we perceive is missing from Act II by going overboard in Act III. This never works. It won't feel organic. Many times, it will feel like you are telling a second story altogether. Keep the pace you set up in Acts I and II and add drama to up the stakes a bit in Act III, and the tension will be there. Don't try to manufacture it and just throw it into the story; readers always know what you are doing when you do this.

The Final Story Check worksheet is a quick check-in to see how things are going. When you write quickly, there may be characters, subplots, and settings that you forget all about. It does happen. That is why you need to make great use of your notes and research sheets. They are vitally important when it comes to rewriting.

FINAL STORY CHECK

Without re-reading it, how does the story feel to you? (Think in terms of flow, pacing, theme, etc.)

Did you leave behind a lot of spelling and grammar issues that are going to need to be corrected?

Does each of your acts have a clear beginning?

Are all your genre elements in place?

Are you happy with your characters, or do you feel you need to work a lot more on characterization?

Does your plot interest you? Are there aspects you don't like?

What do you like about your story?

How will your readers feel by the end?

Did you resolve your main storyline, subplots, and central character arc by the end?

Characters			
Subplots			
Settings			

DAY 29

A shot glass of desire is greater than a pitcher of talent.

—Andy Munthe

OBJECTIVES

- Keep writing if you have not finished; you still have a couple days left!

- Figure out what to do next.

DECIDE WHAT TO DO NEXT

Where do you go from here? Good question! I would suggest you make sure you have all your notes in order. If you want to take a month off to recoup, fine; just make sure you don't forget anything important about your story. Get those notes sheets perfect and keep them in a safe place. *Always* make backup copies of your work, too.

Decide if you want to go into a rewrite of this story right away, or take some time away from it. If you feel you need time away from it, do you need time away from writing altogether? Or do you want to do another BIAM on a different story?

Whatever you decide is fine. Just have a plan of action so you don't lose your momentum. Usually those who write again within a few weeks of the first BIAM continue to write almost every day as a habit. Don't lose the habit!

DAY 30

Desire is the key to motivation, but it's the determination and commitment to an unrelenting pursuit of your goal—a commitment to excellence—that will enable you to attain the success you seek.

—MARIO ANDRETTI

OBJECTIVES

• Rate your BIAM experience so you can fix any issues you have for next time.

• Celebrate your success!

I think the above quote says it all ... and if anyone knows how to move fast, it is Mario Andretti.

RATE YOUR BIAM EXPERIENCE

Take a moment right now to jot down how this process went for you. What did you learn about yourself as a writer? Did you write every day? Did you meet your goal? If not, do you know why? As long as you understand why, you can fix the problem and be successful next time.

Be honest with yourself about the whole thing. If you weren't successful, it might be tempting to think the BIAM program doesn't work (or can't work for you). Perhaps there was one element in BIAM that didn't work for you. If you can honestly say that then, by all means, just drop that element on your next time around. It might seem like BIAM is about rules, rules, rules, but it is really about guiding the writer rather than ruling her. Figure out which elements speak to you and are useful, and then use them and build on them.

If another element isn't as useful to your style of writing, then feel free to adapt or discard it. The only real rule here is that you find a way to get that manuscript finished in a month, and the materials here should help you do just that.

What did you like about this 30-day process, and how were you successful?

What did you not like about this 30-day process, and where do you need improvement?

How can you make the process better for yourself next time? (For instance, should you prepare more, plan to write during different hours, etc.?)

CELEBRATE YOUR BIAM SUCCESS

Go back to the celebration exercise in Week 2. Now is the time to do your celebration! Whatever it was, as long as you reached at least 75 percent of your goal, do it today. Reward yourself. You stuck with it for 30 days, and you deserve some positive reinforcement. You may have fallen a bit short or gone a bit further. It doesn't matter. As long as you are within 75 percent of your goal, you did well. You did more than you probably have done in a long time—right? That deserves a reward.

How does it feel to celebrate?

Everyone wants to be a writer, but few can really claim such a title. But *you* can, because, in the end, it's not publication or recognition that makes someone a writer; it is writing a finished manuscript. If you've stuck with BIAM, and if you have that manuscript, regardless of what's still ahead—polishing, revising, rewriting—then there's one thing you can say now with confidence: You are a *writer*.

Starting manuscripts, playing around with ideas, taking classes, joining groups—these all have their place, for sure, but they don't make you a writer. If someone puts a brush to a canvas, but never finishes a painting, is he a hobbyist, or a painter?

Perseverance, actually sticking with it and finishing your story, is what separates you from the hobbyist and makes you a writer. This is why agents and editors want to see a finished manuscript when it comes to fiction. They want to know you are one of the few who can actually—and who wants to—go the distance.

I know some of you will want to show your work to critics and friends. Be very careful about this. Make sure it is ready to show and be very specific about what you want readers to look for. Make them find at least one positive thing to say. If all you need is support, then tell them you are not looking to find errors; you just want to know if it flows well and seems believable. Again, be specific so you don't open yourself up too much before you are ready. It is best to wait until after at least one rewrite.

Participate in this 30-day plan as often as you like. If you can complete *several* manuscripts, you are well on your way to getting published. Agents and editors love writers who have several finished manuscripts, because they know these writers have worked hard to master their craft and are serious about their careers—that they are not just dreamers or hobbyists.

It really doesn't matter how good or bad this manuscript is. We never had the intention to write a masterpiece in 30 days. It has always been about the journey. I hope you learned a lot about yourself along the way and have grown as a writer. There's always more to learn, so feel free to start the process again.

I wish you much success in your careers and in life. I hope this book has helped you become more successful and has taught you a thing or two along the way. I know I learned a lot from writing it.

WEEK 4 WRAP-UP

- Did your main character successfully reach his intended character arc—the one you mapped out for him on Day 23?

- Is your theme clearly conveyed at the end of your story?

- Is your climactic scene exciting and genre appropriate?

- Did you tie up all your story's loose ends by the resolution?

- Is the ending organic to the story? Did you bring something or someone new in at the last moment to save the day?

- Are you ready for the rewrite? Will you jump right into the rewrite? Take a break? Or work on another story next month?

- Are your research notes up to date as you now prepare for the revision phase?

- Did you complete the exercises on how the process went for you? (Doing so will help prepare you for your next BIAM experience.)

- Did you celebrate your success? Your inner muse is expecting it; don't lie to her.

PROGRESS TRACKER

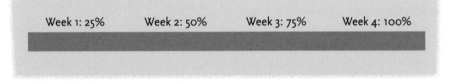

| Week 1: 25% | Week 2: 50% | Week 3: 75% | Week 4: 100% |

WORKSHEET INDEX

STORY TRACKER

ACT I				
Character	Plot	Subplot	Setting	Other

ACT II				
Character	Plot	Subplot	Setting	Other

ACT III				
Character	Plot	Subplot	Setting	Other

WRITING TIME TRACKER
Time Spent Writing Per Day

Project Name:

WEEK 1	1	2	3	4	5	6	7	Totals
Miscellaneous								
Outline								
Act I								
Rewrite								
Word Count								
Distractions								

WEEK 2	8	9	10	11	12	13	14	Totals
Miscellaneous								
Outline								
Act II								
Rewrite								
Word Count								

Book in a Month

Distractions								
WEEK 3	**15**	**16**	**17**	**18**	**19**	**20**	**21**	Totals
Miscellaneous								
Outline								
Act II								
Rewrite								
Word Count								
Distractions								
WEEK 4	**22**	**23**	**24**	**25**	**26**	**27**	**28**	Totals
Miscellaneous								
Outline								
Act III								
Rewrite								
Word Count								
Distractions								

GOAL TRACKER

Goal	Course of Action

BOOK IN A MONTH CONTRACT

Book Title: _____

I,_____ , agree to follow the steps of the 30-day Book in a Month system.

I will make the necessary changes in my life to accommodate this goal, and I will ask family, friends, and my fellow writers for help when I need it. I will organize my time well so I can do this, and I will set aside all non-essential tasks so I have time to achieve my goal.

I will work on my book _____ days a week (if I miss a day, I'll just keep going). I will complete _____ words/pages and get to the end. No matter what happens during these 30 days, I will just keep writing.

"I don't have the time" is not a good enough excuse for the next 30 days.

I promise myself that I will celebrate when the 30 days are up, even if I only met 75 percent of this goal. I will tell my family and friends to get ready for this celebration in Week 3, to further motivate myself.

This book is important to me. My future readers are waiting to read it and I owe it to them to finish it. What I have to say is important.

Signature:_____

Date:_____

STORY IDEA MAP

PLOT

Main Story Idea

Hook/Catalyst/Inciting Incident

Act I Turning Point

The Stakes

CHARACTERS

Major Characters	Minor Characters

SETTING

Setting	Props

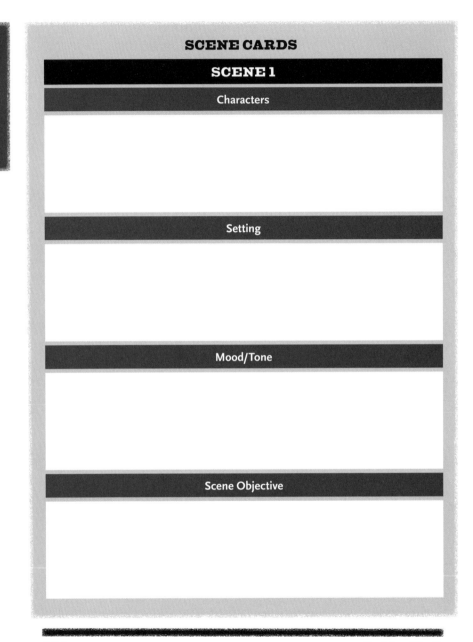

SCENE CARDS

SCENE 1

Characters

Setting

Mood/Tone

Scene Objective

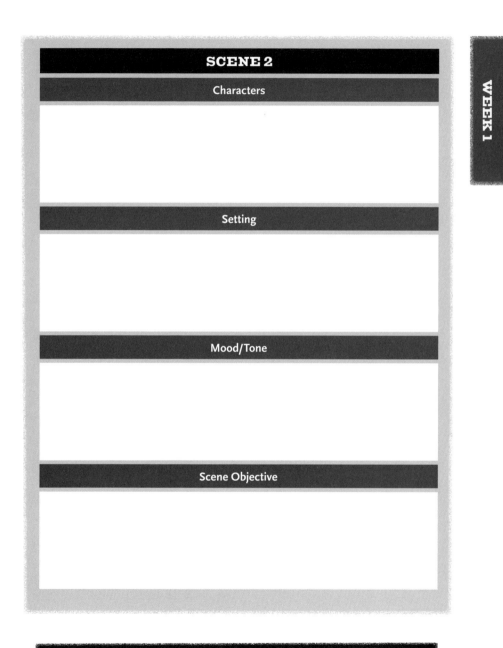

SCENE 2

Characters

Setting

Mood/Tone

Scene Objective

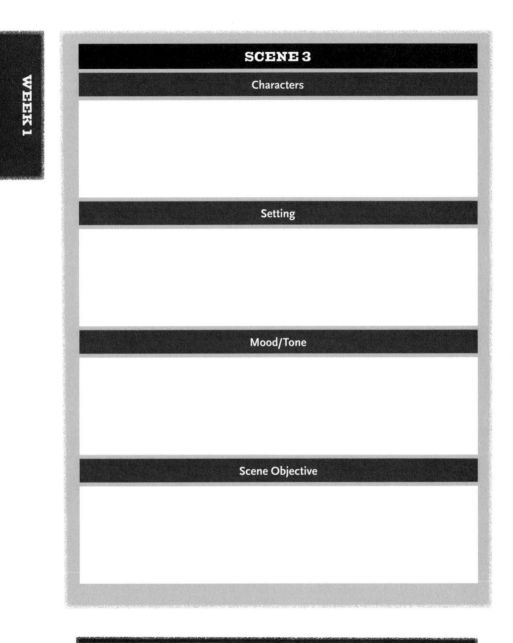

SCENE 3

Characters

Setting

Mood/Tone

Scene Objective

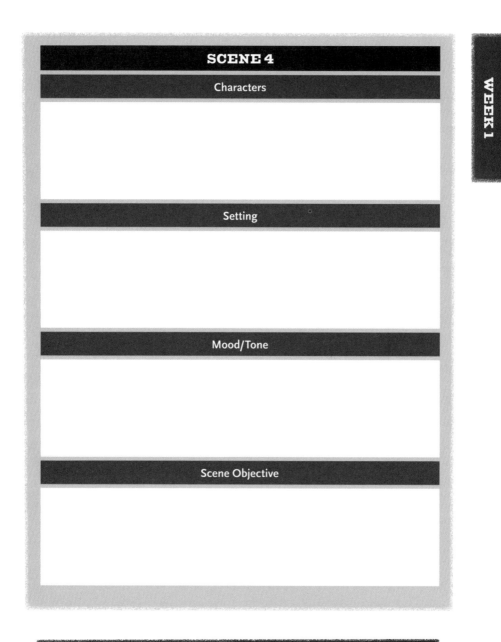

SCENE 4

Characters

Setting

Mood/Tone

Scene Objective

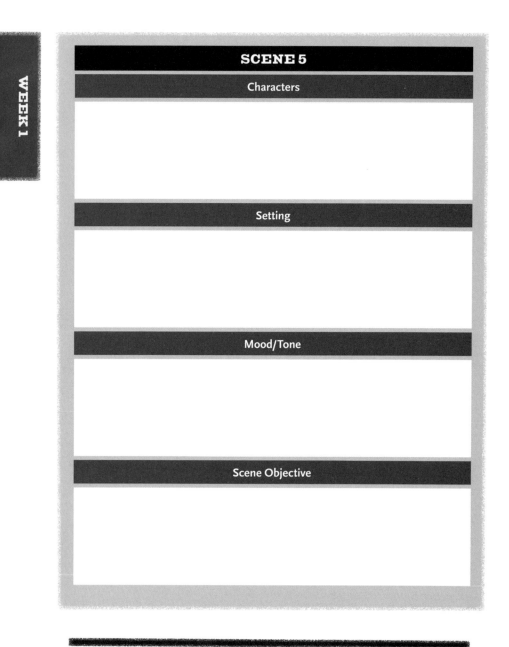

SCENE 5

Characters

Setting

Mood/Tone

Scene Objective

SCENE 6

Characters

Setting

Mood/Tone

Scene Objective

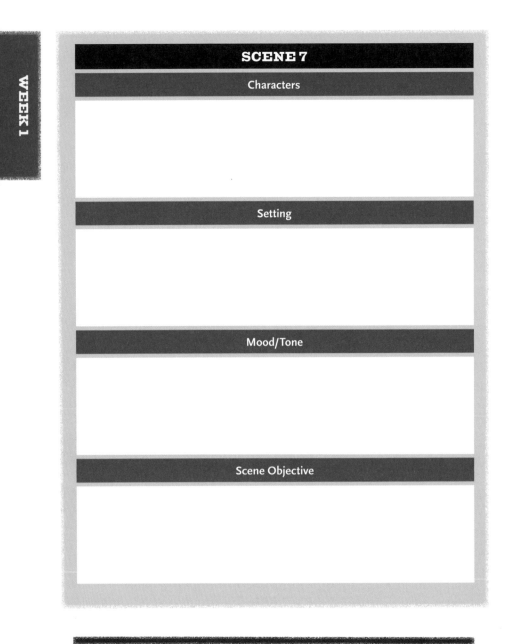

SCENE 7

Characters

Setting

Mood/Tone

Scene Objective

SCENE 8

Characters

Setting

Mood/Tone

Scene Objective

SCENE 9

Characters

Setting

Mood/Tone

Scene Objective

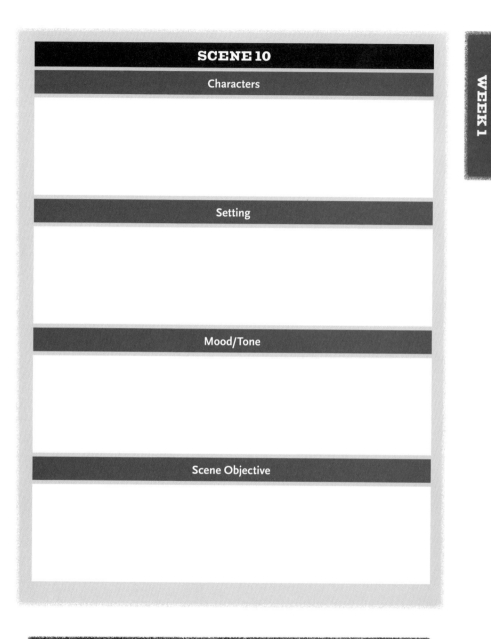

SCENE 10

Characters

Setting

Mood/Tone

Scene Objective

AT-A-GLANCE OUTLINE

TITLE

ACT I (WEEK 1)

Briefly describe what happens in Act I from the initial story hook to the turning point.

Describe the setup.

Describe how the mood or tone is created (props, weather, emotions, setting, characters, style).

Identify the hook/incident.

Identify the first turning point.

Identify what is at stake (why readers should care).

Protagonist's Introduction	Protagonist's Motivation	Details to Remember
Antagonist's Introduction	Antagonist's Motivation	Details to Remember
Supporting Character 1	Supporting Character 2	Unusual Supporting Character
Setting	Props	Time Period

ACT II, PART 1 (WEEK 2)

Briefly describe what happens in the first half of Act II, from where the problem intensifies to the temporary triumph.

Describe how you want readers to feel (mood/tone) when reading this act. Also think about how you want the protagonist to feel.

Describe how the problem intensifies.

Describe the temporary triumph. Is it an inner (psychological) and/or external triumph for the protagonist?

Think about how this triumph can be foreshadowed.

Decide whether a subplot plays a role or causes any effect.

Main Setting for Act II	Other Settings	Props

Any New Characters	Why They Are Needed	Things to Remember

ACT II, PART 2 (WEEK 3)

Briefly describe what happens in the second half of Act II, from the reversal to the second turning point.

Describe how you want readers to feel (mood/tone) when reading this act. Also think about how you want the protagonist to feel.

Describe how you will create and show the reversal.

Describe the second turning point. Think about how it relates to or sets up the final resolution in Act III.

Think about how you can foreshadowed the second turning point in Act I or in the first half of Act II.

Describe how the hero's decisions cause this turning point.

Setting for Second Turning Point	Other Settings Used	Props

New Characters	Why They Are Needed	Things to Remember

ACT III (WEEK 4)

Briefly describe what happens in Act III, from the final obstacle to the resolution.

Describe the final obstacle.

Describe how the mood or tone is created (props, weather, emotions, setting, characters, style).

Describe the climax.

Note any loose ends you might need to tie up in the resolution.

Describe how you want readers to feel when they finish the story.

Think about whether your villain is defeated in the end. If he is, how? What are his crucial mistakes? How are readers likely to respond to his failure or success?

Think about whether your hero wins in the end. If he does, how? What does he learn through his victory or defeat? What is his biggest accomplishment or mistake?

Describe your story's theme.

RESEARCH TRACKER

Topic to Research	What to Look for	Findings

CHARACTER STORY SKETCH

STORY TITLE			CHARACTER NAME		

Age	Ethnicity	Height	Weight	Hair	Eyes

Education	Residence	Job	Archetype	Birth Sign	Religion

Style of Dress	
Distinguishing Marks	

FAVORITE THINGS

Music	Food	Color	Pastime	Entertainment

JUST THE FACTS

Children	
Pets	
Hobbies	

Family Secrets	
Worst Fear	
Greatest Hope	
Skills	
Prized Possession	
Vulnerability	
Regrets	
General Outlook	

GOING DEEPER

Describe the first impression this character makes.

Describe how and why other characters view this character.

Describe what this character needs to learn by the end of the story.

Describe how you will foreshadow this ending in the story's beginning.

CHARACTER SNAPSHOT

VITAL STATISTICS

Name

Nationality

Age

Family Situation

Appearance

Quirks

PSYCHOLOGY

Traumas

Feelings About Settings

Overall Attitude

Fears

Joys

ACCOMPLISHMENTS

Skills

Weaknesses

Awards/Degrees

Dreams/Ambitions

MOTIVATIONS

Top Priorities

Favorite Things/People

Obsessions

Guilts

CHARACTER ARC

Lessons to Learn

Intended Character Changes

IMPORTANT NOTES TO REMEMBER

CHARACTER-REVEALING SCENES

Scenes to reveal appearance:

Scenes to reveal quirks:

Scenes to reveal character's lesson:

Revealing scenes for:

Scenes to reveal skills/ weaknesses:

Scenes to reveal motivation:

Scenes to reveal trauma:

ACT I TURNING POINT BRAINSTORM

What is the exact opposite that could happen at this turning point?

What is the most outrageous thing that could happen at this point?

What would happen if you brought in another character?

How do you want readers to react or feel at this point?

BACKSTORY BRAINSTORM

Backstory for Me	Backstory to Include	Relevance to Frontstory	Possible Scene Locations

CHARACTER MOTIVATORS

Scene	Character	Flaws and Goals	Resistance	Direct Motivation

WEEK 2

PLOT SNAPSHOT

Describe, in detail, the first event that happens in this story.

Describe what this event accomplishes. (Does it advance plot, reveal character, make readers feel specific emotions, etc.?)

Setting	Characters Involved	Conflicts That Arise and Their Effect

Describe how the conflicts that arise affect the characters and plot in both the short- and long-term of your story.

Describe, in detail, the second event that happens in this story.

Describe what this event accomplishes.

Setting	Characters Involved	Conflicts That Arise and Their Effect

Describe how the conflicts that arise affect the characters and plot in both the short- and long-term of your story.

Describe, in detail, the third event that happens in this story.

Describe what this event accomplishes.

Setting	Characters Involved	Conflicts That Arise

Describe how the conflicts that arise affect the characters and plot in both the short- and long-term of your story.

* Remember that every plot should have at least three big events, regardless of if it is a character- or plot-driven story.

WEEK 2

CLIFFHANGER BRAINSTORM

Identify and describe a scene in the first part of Act II that has cliffhanger potential.

Quickly outline three cliffhanger ideas and their resolutions.

For each idea, describe what you will cut to immediately after the cliffhanger.

For each idea, describe how you will return to the cliffhanger to resolve it.

Describe how each cliffhanger option will affect your characters and your plot both in the short- and long-term of your story.

PLOT BRAINSTORM

What specifically in Act II will make your readers care about the hero's goal?

What interests you most about Act II? (Something better!)

What is the wildest thing that can happen as Act II progresses?

If you had to shock your readers in Act II, what could you do?

What are three different turning points you might throw into Act II to keep it interesting (if needed)?

CHARACTER BRAINSTORM

How will your main character grow (or perhaps resist change) in Act II?

What fears will your main character have to overcome in Act II?

Which supporting characters will play a major role in Act II, and how?

Will any new characters be introduced in Act II? If so, why? How will you foreshadow them?

What does your main character do differently in Act II?

Does your main character show another side of himself in Act II—a side that has always been there, but readers may not have really noticed before? If so, do you properly fore-shadow this in Act I?

Soon your main character will be facing the final confrontation; is he up to it yet, or does he have more to learn in Act II?

Book in a Month

Will your main character have to lie or cheat in Act II?

What have you learned about your character's ethics by Act II? Would he swear? Would he hurt one to save many? How far would he go to get the job done?

If your character's house were burning down, what object do you think he would save? Why?

What event in Act II makes your character question whether his goal is really worth it, and why? What motivates him onward in spite of this doubt?

How could the antagonist have a bigger presence in Act II?

Does the antagonist have any phobias, weaknesses, or shortcomings that come out in Act II?

SETTING BRAINSTORM

What props could you put into Act II to spice it up?

Does the setting affect the plot progression in Act II at all? Does it cause any additional obstacles?

Is there a new setting you can introduce in Act II?

Can you change a setting in Act II and throw the characters off? (For instance, the bank they planned to rob has been turned into a restaurant, and all their plans to break into the safe are foiled.)

Have new characters taken over a setting in Act II? (For example, the government has occupied a town, and now the hero can't pass the checkpoints to reach his destination.)

CONFLICT BRAINSTORM

	Scene	Characters Involved	Result
Barrier			
Complication			
Situation			
Barrier			
Complication			
Situation			

WEEK 2

TEMPORARY TRIUMPH BRAINSTORM

Scene	Characters Involved	Temporary Triumph	Reversal	Ramifications (Long- and Short-Term)

SUBPLOT BRAINSTORM

Subplot	Function	Characters Involved	Subplot Resolution

THE DOMINO SCENE TEST

Scene Summary	Scene Connector	Scene Summary

THEME SPIDER

Why you wrote this story:	What you like about this story:	What you want readers to get:
Props used to express your theme:	**Theme:**	How your main character and theme are connected:
Places where your theme is too overt or too subtle:		Scenes crucial to conveying your theme:
Personal message you want your story to convey:	Choices made to ensure your theme gets conveyed:	Notes:

SCENE SEQUENCER

SEQUENCE SYNOPSIS

Beginning	Setting	Characters	Crucial Elements

Middle	Setting	Characters	Crucial Elements

End	Setting	Characters	Crucial Elements

REVERSAL BRAINSTORM

CURRENT REVERSAL

	How This Would Alter the Current Reversal
New Information	
New Situation	
Unexpected Betrayals	
Unexpected Shows of Support	
Last-Minute Change of Plans	
Change of Heart	
Change in Perceptions	

WEEK 3

GENRE ELEMENTS TRACKER

ACT I	ACT II	ACT III
Element	Element	Element
Characters	Characters	Characters
Props or Items Used	Props or Items Used	Props or Items Used
Intended Reader Response	Intended Reader Response	Intended Reader Response
Other Notes	Other Notes	Other Notes

VILLAIN BRAINSTORM

Redeeming Qualities	Skills	Weaknesses

ACT II TURNING POINT BRAINSTORM

What is the exact opposite that could happen at this turning point?

What is the most outrageous thing that could happen at this point?

What would happen if you brought in another character?

How do you want readers to react or feel at this point?

HERO'S STORY COMPASS

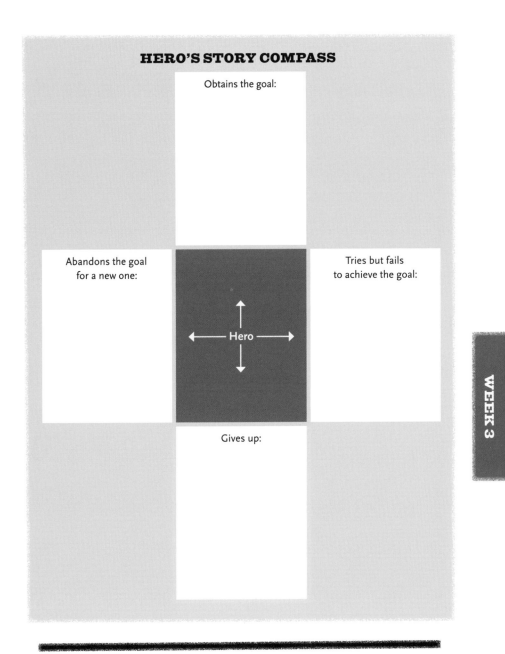

Obtains the goal:

Abandons the goal
for a new one:

Hero

Tries but fails
to achieve the goal:

Gives up:

HERO REWARD GLANCE

Hero's Original Motivation

Obstacles Overcome

Obstacles Still to Come

Intended Story Resolution

Reward Options

1.

2.

3.

WEEK 3

VILLAIN REWARD GLANCE

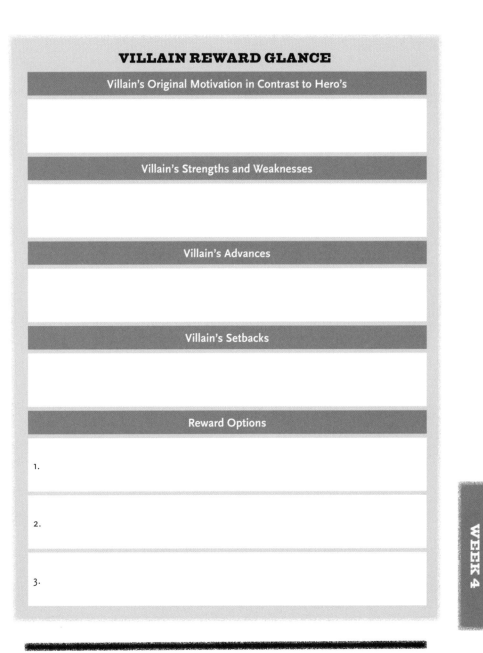

Villain's Original Motivation in Contrast to Hero's

Villain's Strengths and Weaknesses

Villain's Advances

Villain's Setbacks

Reward Options

1.

2.

3.

CHARACTER ARC TRACKER

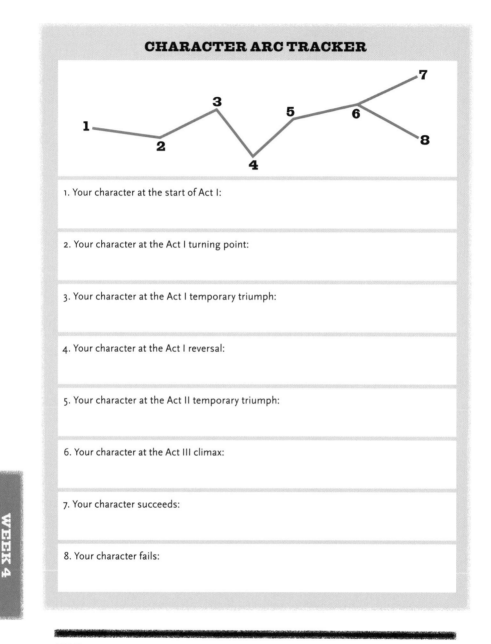

1. Your character at the start of Act I:

2. Your character at the Act I turning point:

3. Your character at the Act I temporary triumph:

4. Your character at the Act I reversal:

5. Your character at the Act II temporary triumph:

6. Your character at the Act III climax:

7. Your character succeeds:

8. Your character fails:

FINAL OBSTACLE BRAINSTORM

Act I Turning Point

Act II Turning Point

Story Compass Selection

Hero's Intended Arc

Final Obstacle Options

1.

2.

3.

4.

CLIMAX BRAINSTORM

Final Obstacle Recap

Characters

Setting and Props

Genre Considerations

Climax Options

1.

2.

3.

4.

THEME REVELATION CHECK

Intended Theme

Act I Theme Reinforcers

Act II Theme Reinforcers

Act III Theme Reinforcers

Theme Resolution Options

1.

2.

3.

RESOLUTION BRAINSTORM

Plot Resolution	Subplot Resolution	Character Resolution

Book in a Month

FINAL STORY CHECK

Without re-reading it, how does the story feel to you? (Think in terms of flow, pacing, theme, etc.)

Did you leave behind a lot of spelling and grammar issues that are going to need to be corrected?

Does each of your acts have a clear beginning?

Are all your genre elements in place?

Are you happy with your characters, or do you feel you need to work a lot more on characterization?

Does your plot interest you? Are there aspects you don't like?

What do you like about your story?

How will your readers feel by the end?

Did you resolve your main storyline, subplots, and central character arc by the end?

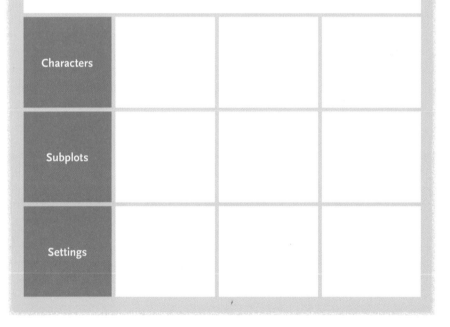

Characters			
Subplots			
Settings			